"The great strength of this book lies in the organization, pract presentation, which both newly-qualified and experienced clinicians can adapt to their therapeutic practice with children."

—*Associate Professor Lesley Bretherton, Royal Children's Hospital, Melbourne, Australia*

"An excellent guide…based on clinical experience and practical, engaging methods. It promotes a thoughtful orientation to working with children and includes a broad range of creative activities."

—*Professor Vicki Anderson, Head of Psychology, Royal Children's Hospital, Melbourne, Australia*

"This should be a very helpful handbook for the child mental health field."

—*Professor Margot Prior, Honorary Professor, Melbourne School of Psychological Sciences, University of Melbourne, Australia*

"This is an essential handbook for mental health professionals working collaboratively and respectfully with children and their families. It outlines playful therapeutic approaches to help children identify and communicate difficult feelings and to develop effective coping strategies."

—*Dr Deborah Hutchins, Clinical Psychologist, Royal Children's Hospital, Melbourne, Australia of related interest*

More Creative Coping Skills for Children
Activities, Games, Stories, and Handouts to
Help Children Self-regulate
Bonnie Thomas
ISBN 978 1 78592 021 9
eISBN 978 1 78450 267 6

Inspiring and Creative Ideas for Working with Children
How to Build Relationships and Enable Change
Deborah M. Plummer
ISBN 978 1 84905 651 9
eISBN 978 1 78450 146 4

The School of Wellbeing
12 Extraordinary Projects Promoting Children and
Young People's Mental Health and Happiness
Jenny Hulme
ISBN 978 1 78592 096 7
eISBN 978 1 78450 359 8

Promoting Young Children's Emotional Health and Wellbeing
A Practical Guide for Professionals and Parents
Sonia Mainstone-Cotton
ISBN 978 1 78592 054 7
eISBN 978 1 78450 311 6

**101 Mindful Arts-Based Activities to Get
Children and Adolescents Talking**
Working with Severe Trauma, Abuse and
Neglect Using Found and Everyday Objects
Dawn D'Amico
ISBN 978 1 78592 731 7
eISBN 978 1 78450 422 9

**The Big Book of EVEN MORE Therapeutic
Activity Ideas for Children and Teens**
Inspiring Arts-Based Activities and Character Education Curricula
Lindsey Joiner
ISBN 978 1 84905 749 3
eISBN 978 1 78450 196 9

Be the Jellyfish Training Manual
Supporting Children's Social and Emotional Wellbeing
Lucy Cree and Sarah Brogden
ISBN 978 1 78592 242 8
eISBN 978 1 78450 522 6

CREATIVE WAYS TO
HELP CHILDREN MANAGE
BIG FEELINGS

A THERAPIST'S GUIDE TO WORKING WITH PRESCHOOL AND PRIMARY CHILDREN

DR FIONA ZANDT AND **DR SUZANNE BARRETT**

FOREWORD BY ASSOCIATE PROFESSOR LESLEY BRETHERTON

Jessica Kingsley *Publishers*
London and Philadelphia

First published in 2017
by Jessica Kingsley Publishers
73 Collier Street
London N1 9BE, UK
and
400 Market Street, Suite 400
Philadelphia, PA 19106, USA

www.jkp.com

Library of Congress Cataloging in Publication Data
A CIP catalog record for this book is available from the Library of Congress

British Library Cataloguing in Publication Data
Title: Creative ways to help children manage BIG feelings : a therapist's guide to working with preschool and primary children / Dr Fiona Zandt and Dr Suzanne Barrett.
Description: London ; Philadelphia : Jessica Kingsley Publishers, 2017. | Includes bibliographical references and index.
Identifiers: LCCN 2016046980 (print) | LCCN 2016048872 (ebook) | ISBN 9781785920745 (alk. paper) | ISBN 9781784504878 (ebook)
Subjects: | MESH: Psychotherapy--methods | Child
Classification: LCC RJ504 (print) | LCC RJ504 (ebook) | NLM WS 350.2 | DDC
   618.92/8914--dc23
LC record available at https://lccn.loc.gov/2016046980

ISBN 978 1 78592 074 5
eISBN 978 1 78450 487 8

Printed and bound in the United States

To James, Joseph, Christian and Edith—
my greatest loves and best teachers.

FZ

To Arch, Alyssa, Annabelle and Bradley—
for all the love, joy and wisdom you bring to my life.

SB

Contents

Foreword

Children use play from an early age; it helps them to develop confidence and resilience and allows them to share, negotiate and problem solve with peers and others; importantly, it promotes a joyful childhood. The authors of this book, both clinical psychologists, have harnessed children's love of play to provide an invaluable therapeutic resource for clinicians. The outcome is a user-friendly guide to a host of developmentally appropriate creative and, importantly, fun activities to assist with the therapeutic process in children with social, emotional and behavioral problems.

The great strength of this book lies in the organization, practical format and respectful presentation, which both newly-qualified and experienced clinicians can adapt to their therapeutic practice with children. Part I stresses the importance of a strong evidence base when assessing, diagnosing, formulating and sharing a treatment plan. The authors encourage creativity in the therapist but stress the importance of remaining true to a strong theoretical framework and provide a multitude of references for their assertions. Of even greater value is the significance given to the developmental considerations when working with children, and this is where Part II of the book comes into its own.

Part II is a logically organized set of creative activities, provided in an easily accessible format, which therapists can adapt according to the age, developmental level and interest of the child. The availability of the parent is also respectfully considered. The activities follow a set format: a short introduction, the materials required, how to go about the activity, how to involve parents and what to consider in terms of the child's development; possible adaptations are often considered. Some old favorites are presented—for example, *Big volcano*—but there are plenty of new activities as well, often tapping into the current popular culture for children. However, this is not a manual to slavishly follow. The therapist is encouraged to select and perhaps adapt activities following a thorough assessment and formulation and as part of the implementation of an evidence-based treatment plan. In other words, Part I is integral to Part II.

Overall, while the book is primarily aimed at psychologists, it will appeal to a range of clinicians working with children. Therapists with a range of experience from newly qualified to 'old hands' will be able to customize a list of favorite activities and apply these in their work with children who present with feelings of worry, sadness, fear or anger. This is an engaging resource based on solid evidence and clinical acumen by two experienced clinical psychologists and, while it is a wonderful addition to child psychology, it will also appeal to and enhance the therapeutic practice in a range of professionals working with children.

Associate Professor Lesley Bretherton
The Royal Children's Hospital, Melbourne, Australia

Acknowledgements

We would like to thank all the families who have allowed us to share their journey. Their courage, wisdom and ability to find humor in difficult situations is inspiring.

We would also like to thank our colleagues and friends for their helpful feedback in the preparation of this book. In particular we would like to thank Associate Professor Lesley Bretherton, Dr Deborah Hutchins, Professor Margot Prior, Professor Vicki Anderson, Fran Craig, Elissa Notley and Nicole Francke for their advice and support.

Preface

The essence of this book is about using play to introduce therapeutic concepts to children and provide a space in which they can explore these ideas. Having a playful approach to therapy helps to engage children and assists them to understand and utilize therapeutic concepts. Being playful also makes therapy fun for children and parents, as well as therapists. It is our hope that this book provides you with some new ideas for working therapeutically with children and inspires you to develop some creative activities of your own.

This book focuses on helping children who are struggling with feelings of worry, fear, sadness or anger. While we expect that all children experience these feelings, some children will struggle more than others. For some children, their feelings will be too big for them to manage alone. Many of these children will meet the criteria for an anxiety disorder, a depressive episode, or a behavioral disorder and a large number will have more than one disorder.

Appropriate assessment, formulation and diagnosis is essential for working therapeutically with children; however, we have not organized this book according to diagnostic categories. There are several reasons for this. First, around a third of children who meet the criteria for an emotional or behavioral disorder will also meet the criteria for another disorder (Ford, Goodman and Meltzer 2003; Lawrence *et al.* 2015). Second, working therapeutically with children who have anxiety, mood or behavioral difficulties has many commonalities. For example, children with both anxiety and depression often struggle with emotional regulation and unhelpful thinking patterns, and lack coping strategies. Finally, in our experience, different emotional and behavioral difficulties can be interrelated. For example, angry outbursts are commonly triggered by situations that make the child feel anxious, and can result in challenging behaviors.

Like most experienced therapists our style is eclectic, drawing on a number of theoretical approaches. A developmental perspective sits as our overriding framework, which guides us in modifying therapy for the children we work with. Our approach is strongly influenced by our training in, and many years of using, cognitive behavioral therapy with children. A systemic family focus also guides our understanding of children and families and permeates our therapy. In addition, we draw on concepts and interventions from acceptance and commitment therapy and narrative therapy, and incorporate these when relevant. We use play to engage children and to introduce therapeutic concepts and strategies. Our approach fits well with cognitive behavioral play therapy, an approach described by Knell (2015) as using cognitive and behavioral interventions within a structured play therapy framework.

We believe that a strong theoretical basis is important in therapy work, and we provide a brief overview of each of the therapeutic frameworks that influence our work in the first chapter. Your own theoretical basis, however, does not have to be an exact match to ours. Instead, we encourage you to incorporate our ideas and activities into your own framework, whether it is a traditional cognitive behavioral therapy framework, or more strongly influenced by behavior therapy, acceptance and commitment therapy, family therapy, narrative therapy, or any directive play therapy approach.

However, this is not a therapy manual and it assumes a basic knowledge of these therapies. Rather, the activities included in this book are more like a treasure trove of ideas that you can sift and sort through using your clinical knowledge and your understanding of your client, choosing what is appropriate.

Creativity is central to our work with children. Ronen (1997) wrote that "therapists who treat children, unlike other therapists, need to be artistic—in their capacity to be flexible, creative, and interesting" (p.xviii). Being able to modify therapy to meet a child's needs, adjusting the activity so that it fits with their developmental level, and engaging them by utilizing topics and methods that suit their interests is a constant challenge. Meeting this challenge requires therapists to be flexible and creative both when planning their sessions and when responding to children within sessions.

This book was developed from workshops we facilitated, the focus of which was working creatively with children. The workshops were aimed at child therapists with a background in psychology, social work, and other relevant professions. Initially we aimed the workshops at newly-qualified therapists; however, we had many experienced therapists attend and we realized that they too found it useful.

The first part of this book outlines our approach to working with children, while the second includes activities that we often find useful in our work. Each of the activities is presented simply, with a clear aim, list of materials and a method. Many of the activities also include variations and ideas for extension.

While it might be tempting to read the activities alone, we would strongly urge you to read the first part of the book too. The activities in this book are only therapeutic when implemented in the context of a thorough treatment plan following a comprehensive assessment by an appropriately trained professional. Reading the first part will enable you to develop a good grounding in child therapy if you are new to the area and help you to put the activities that follow into context.

If you are an experienced therapist reading this book then we would strongly encourage you to read the first part of this book too, reviewing your practice as you do so. As experienced therapists we love having students and supervisees. In providing them with guidance and answering their questions we find ourselves reviewing and reflecting on our own practice. It has been wonderful to see what experienced therapists have taken from our workshops. Some have left reflecting on basic elements of their practice, such as how they can work more with parents, incorporate some family sessions into their practice, or even how they can set up the physical space in their clinic room so that it facilitates a more playful approach to therapy.

With a few exceptions, the activities included in the second part of this book have been developed in our work with clients. To the best of our knowledge these activities are originals and are not used elsewhere. That said, the ideas are simple ones, and it is possible that you or others have developed similar ways of working with children. The few exceptions are several activities that are commonly used in therapy, including *Blow your worries away*, *Body mapping*, *Calm box*, *Fear hierarchy* and *Feelings thermometer*. Although similar activities are used in other programs, we felt it essential to include them here as they really are a core part of working with children. We have described the way in which we present and use these activities with children, including our tips and variations that we have found helpful. Wherever we have been aware of a similar activity or approach we have made reference to it so that you can read further if you wish to do so.

In developing activities, we have attempted to use materials that are inexpensive and readily available, meaning that you do not need to invest time and money in specialty shopping. We are mindful that many of you will work across settings and therefore need to rely on materials that don't take up a lot of space and can be easily transported. We are also conscious that therapists, particularly those who are in the early stages of their careers, often do not have large sums of money to spend on specialist resources. Most of the activities use simple materials such as paper and markers, cardboard boxes, a ball, play-doh, or glass jars.

All of the activities in this book are designed to be used by psychologists, social workers, mental health clinicians and other appropriately qualified and experienced professionals. The activities should be used following a thorough assessment, as one component of an overall treatment plan. As always, we urge you to use your clinical judgment in your work with children and their families and to engage in appropriate supervision. Your own clinical decision-making regarding each individual client is essential in choosing an appropriate therapeutic approach and activities at each stage of therapy. Clinical skill is required to be able to modify the activities provided here to your individual client and use these in a thoughtful and collaborative manner, responding in the moment to the child in front of you.

Within this book we use the word therapist to refer to the psychologist, social worker, counsellor, psychotherapist, or other mental health clinician. The word "child" refers to the client, with the emphasis in this book being on preschool- and primary school-aged children. The word "parent" refers to anyone who is in the role of a caregiver or guardian. There are a number of case examples used in the first part of the book. The details in each case have been altered substantially to ensure the privacy of children and families and they have been chosen because they represent common patterns we have observed in children over the years.

We begin Part I by briefly outlining the therapeutic frameworks that inform our work and reflecting on the ways in which working with children differs from working with adults. We then focus in Chapter 2 on the importance of assessment, including some practical ideas relevant for assessing children and families. In the chapters that follow, we begin to explore therapy with children in more detail. This includes a discussion of how to ensure therapy is purposeful, the use of play in therapy, and working with parents, families and preschools or schools. We also look more specifically at the preschool and the primary school periods from a developmental perspective and consider how therapy needs to be modified for children in these age groups and to take into account developmental concerns. We finish Part I of the book by describing some of the core components of child therapy, including many practical and helpful ideas, and finally outlining how to use the activities in this book.

Therapeutic Work with Children and Families

CHAPTER 1

Therapeutic Frameworks and Why Working with Children Is Different

This chapter provides an overview of the major therapeutic frameworks that influence our work with children. We consider the importance of a developmental perspective and look at some of the key ways in which working with children differs to working with adults.

Therapeutic frameworks

Our approach fits within a cognitive behavioral therapy framework, though modified to be developmentally appropriate for children, with a systemic family focus and a playful context. We also incorporate elements of narrative therapy and acceptance and commitment therapy. We will briefly outline each of these therapeutic frameworks and supporting research here.

Cognitive behavioral therapy

Cognitive behavioral therapy (CBT) focuses on helping children to understand the relationship between their thoughts, feelings and behavior. It involves interventions aimed at identifying and changing unhelpful thoughts that impact on the child's emotions and behaviors, as well as behavioral techniques such as exposure and behavioral experiments or skills training. CBT is a well-established therapy for the adult population; however, there has been a clear recognition that CBT needs to be modified for use with children (Knell 2015; Ronen 1997; Stallard 2013). Kendall was one of the pioneers of CBT with children and his books on the subject continue to be among the most helpful (for example see Kendall 2006a).

There is good support for the efficacy of CBT in treating emotional and behavioral difficulties in school-aged children and adolescents (for reviews see David-Ferdon and Kaslow 2008; Eyberg, Nelson and Boggs 2008; Silverman, Pina and Viswesvaran 2008). A number of CBT programs have been developed specifically for children, such as the Cool Kids program (Rapee *et al.* 2006) and the Friends program, which originated with an Australian adaptation of Kendall's Coping Cat program (see Barrett 1999). CBT workbooks, including psychoeducational material and worksheets, have also been developed for older children (e.g. Huebner 2005, 2007a, 2007b; Stallard 2002). More recently, CBT programs for younger, preschool-aged children have been developed (e.g. Fun FRIENDS Program; Barrett, Fisak and Cooper 2015) and some research has emerged supporting the efficacy of CBT in treating this younger age group (Barrett *et al.* 2015; Hirshfeld-Becker *et al.* 2011; Pahl and Barrett 2010). We discuss this further in Chapter 5.

The development of cognitive behavioral play therapy is a recent example of CBT being modified to better meet the needs of children (see Knell 2015). It was developed by adapting empirically supported cognitive and behavioral techniques for use in a play setting with preschool and early school-aged children. Knell (2015) describes some key elements of cognitive behavioral play therapy. As the name suggests, children are involved in therapy through play, and that therapy focuses on the child's thoughts, feelings, fantasies and environment, and includes strategies for developing more adaptive thoughts and behaviors. One aspect of this approach that clearly differentiates it from other play therapy approaches is that it is directive and goal-driven, with structured components. Many of the interventions discussed in this book are derived from a CBT framework but delivered through play, and in that way could be considered cognitive behavioral play therapy.

Play therapy

Play therapy was pioneered by therapists such as Anna Freud and Melanie Klein and has a long tradition in being used to treat children with a broad range of emotional and behavioral difficulties. Play is utilized as the child's language and the assumption is that children will symbolically enact or draw feelings and experiences that they cannot put into words. Although play therapy is often criticized for lacking an empirical basis, a meta-analysis by Bratton and colleagues in 2005 reviewed 93 controlled studies and found that play therapy was effective, with the inclusion of parents leading to better outcomes. The criticisms were further disputed by Bratton (2015), who reviews recent research into play therapy and concludes that although limitations exist, there is considerable evidence that play therapy is an effective intervention for children with a range of emotional and behavioral difficulties.

Acceptance and commitment therapy

Acceptance and commitment therapy (ACT) is a newer CBT approach that encourages the development of mindfulness and acceptance of inner experiences, such as thoughts and feelings, rather than trying to change, avoid or cling to them. ACT also focuses on helping individuals identify what is important and meaningful to them, to promote behavior change that will lead to improved quality of life. Hayes and Ciarrochi (2015) have recently presented a model for using ACT with youth which has been modified to provide developmentally appropriate concepts and interventions. Research into the effectiveness of ACT with adolescents is in its preliminary stages, though the studies to date have shown promising results (Hayes, Boyd and Sewell 2011; Livheim *et al.* 2015). With children, however, research has yet to clearly demonstrate the effectiveness of ACT (for a recent review see Swain *et al.* 2015).

One of the elements of ACT that we find helpful in our work with clients is the emphasis on trying out new behaviors and focusing on what really matters. Understanding that even difficult thoughts and emotions are transient is also useful for children and parents. This concept is consistent with the practice of mindfulness, which is a component of ACT but has a longer history and is widely used outside of ACT. Mindfulness has been defined as bringing awareness and attention directly to the present-moment experience of thoughts, feelings and sensations (Willard 2010). The use of mindfulness with children at school, home and in therapy has been growing in popularity and we talk further about our clinical use of mindfulness in Chapter 6. Although mindfulness training has been gaining support for its efficacy with adults, research with children is only in its early stages (Burke 2010; Zelazo and Lyons 2011).

Narrative therapy

Narrative therapy uses play and storytelling to help children develop a coherent narrative of their experiences. Actively engaging in storytelling allows the child to take control and develop the storyline in their preferred manner and provides opportunities to expand and change the story. Narrative approaches enable children to distance themselves through pretense. Michael White, an experienced Australian family therapist, developed narrative therapy and identified four main stages in which children can be engaged in externalizing a problem. White described externalizing conversations as involving defining and naming the problem, mapping the effects of the problem, evaluating the effects of the problem and justifying the evaluation (White and Morgan 2006). Externalizing conversations can also be used for exploring people's strengths, resources, and relationships, as well as the problems they experience (White and Morgan 2006). Ann Cattanach has written a number of books on the use of narrative therapy (for example, see Cattanach 2008).

Narrative therapy is a widely used family therapy approach. While family therapy and family-based interventions are well supported by research, Carr (2014b) comments that more research is needed on narrative approaches. In our clinical work with children and families, we have found the concept of externalizing the problem as separate from the child to be very helpful. We often utilize externalizing conversations in our work, frequently beginning these conversations at the time of assessment.

Family therapy

Family therapy has a long tradition and its emphasis on family relationships and on the broader system make it particularly useful when working with children. Family interactions are observed and the structure within the family is considered. Systems theory proposes that an individual's problem or difficulty needs to be understood in the context of the family and the broader system in which the family fits (Nichols 2011). Different schools of family therapy emphasize different aspects of family relationships in order to facilitate change. Nichols (2011) provides a good overview, as do Goldenberg and Goldenberg (2013) and Carr (2012).

There is a growing body of literature supporting the effectiveness of family therapy in treating childhood mood, anxiety and disruptive behavior disorders (see Carr 2012, 2014a, and Kaslow *et al.* 2012 for reviews). Carr (2014a) presents evidence from meta-analyses, systematic literature reviews and controlled trials demonstrating the effectiveness of systemic interventions for families of children with various emotional and behavioral disorders. He used a broad definition of systemic interventions by including family therapy and other family-based approaches such as parent training, and support was found for these when used either alone or alongside other treatment modalities (for example, alongside individual therapy with the children, or interventions with the broader system such as the school). He noted systemic interventions developed within the cognitive behavioral tradition were well supported. Retzlaff *et al.* (2013) and von Sydow *et al.* (2013) provide recent reviews that focus specifically on systemic family therapy, finding good support for its efficacy in treating childhood emotional and behavioral difficulties.

Beyond therapeutic frameworks

Therapeutic frameworks provide a basis; however, a developmental approach is central to our work with children. Having good relationships with children and families is also essential to our work, regardless of the therapeutic frameworks we employ.

The importance of a developmental perspective

Our understanding of child development provides an important framework influencing our work with children and families. A developmental perspective underlies all of our work with children regardless of the therapeutic frameworks we use. Having a clear understanding of a child's abilities is essential to being able to provide developmentally appropriate therapy. This includes knowing what skills a child has developed and which are currently emerging. For this reason, having a good understanding of what is typical for children at each age and stage is essential. Beyond this, though, therapists who work with children need to be able to gauge a child's development, recognizing that individual children vary. Therapists also need to be mindful of developmental delays and problems and may need to complete formal assessments or refer to other clinicians for assessment.

A developmental perspective is also relevant to the way in which we understand and support families. Being able to consider the developmental level of each of the family members often helps to understand the presenting problem. Consider Ned, a nine-year-old boy who is the eldest of two children in an intact family. Ned experienced anxiety around separation and was reluctant to be alone in his room. Having his younger sister offer to go and get his toys from his room for him generated a range of feelings and impacted on their relationship. His mother feels anxious about her ability to parent school-aged children, having had a difficult relationship with their own parents over this time. Ned's father had just taken a promotion, worked long hours and generally did not see the children on weekdays. As is apparent in this example, having a developmental perspective enables the clinician to better understand a child's difficulties in the context of the family.

We explore developmental theory in more specific detail in Chapter 5, though its influence will be apparent throughout the book.

The importance of relationships

While the therapeutic frameworks shape our work, the relationships we develop with children and families form an essential base for therapy. Developing and maintaining a good rapport with children and families throughout therapy is important and often seems more crucial than the particular approach we take. Shirk and Karver (2003) found that the therapeutic relationship was associated with outcome when working with children and adolescents, regardless of the type of treatment or age of the child. A further meta-analysis revealed that the therapist's interpersonal and direct influence skills, as well as the willingness of the young person and their parents to participate in therapy, and the actual involvement of the young person and their parents in the therapy process, have been shown to be the greatest predictors of outcome (Karver *et al.* 2006). More recently, Cummings *et al.* (2013) found that a strong therapeutic relationship was associated with positive outcome in children and adolescents with anxiety who received CBT.

We often reflect on the relationships we are developing with children and families and also encourage our students and supervisees to consider this. Developing relationships that are respectful and honest sounds simple; however, in practice, therapists can find this difficult. Similarly, developing a good relationship with a therapist can be difficult for families, particularly for those who have experienced trauma or have previously found therapy to be unhelpful. Parents who have a history of attachment difficulties or their own mental health issues can also find it challenging to develop a therapeutic relationship.

Why working with children is different

Working with children is very different to working with adults for a range of reasons. Having a good understanding of these differences is essential for inexperienced therapists as well as those who have previously worked with adults and are moving to working with children. Some of the key reasons that working with children is different are that children are brought to therapy, they are part of a system and they are still developing.

Children are brought to therapy

It is important to remember that children are brought to therapy. They do not come of their own choosing and may not perceive there to be a difficulty. Further, they may have little investment in doing anything differently. Sometimes children may resent their parents for bringing them and resent you for taking up time that they might otherwise spend doing what they enjoy. Kendall (2006b) explains that it is therefore important that the child's initial experience of therapy is enjoyable and positive and helps them to see the possible benefits of therapy.

Sometimes children have had very little warning that they will be attending therapy and have little or no awareness of what therapy entails. We have certainly had children come to the first appointment without knowing where they are being taken. This can be very distressing for a child and presents a challenge to engagement. It is often helpful to have provided some written information to the family about what they can say to their child about coming to see you. We also like to ask the child when they arrive what they have been told about coming. This provides an opportunity to clarify any misconceptions and to describe your role in a child-friendly manner. For example, we would state our name and explain that it is our job to see children who are having a bit of a hard time. We would then explain that these children might be having a hard time at school or home and might be worried or angry, varying what we say depending upon the child's presenting problem. Explaining a little about the process of therapy is helpful. For example, we might say that first we are going to get to know each other a little and come up with some ideas about what might help. It is important to convey a sense of hope so we typically note that most children who come to see us go away feeling a lot better. Often this can lead into a discussion about confidentiality, which is discussed in further detail in Chapter 5.

Most often it is parents who bring their children to therapy. Implicit in this is the notion that the child is experiencing a problem and that this problem needs to be fixed. Part of our assessment, however, is about seeing the child's difficulties within the context of the family and this can be a shift for many families. Parents may be surprised to learn that they are expected to participate actively in therapy and benefit from having a clear rationale about why this is important. Ensuring that parents feel empowered by the knowledge that they can do something different rather than feeling blamed is essential to therapy.

Sometimes parents feel that they are being brought—or sent—to therapy too. A school teacher may have strongly recommended seeing a therapist or another professional might have made the referral. In these situations, even though the therapy is not mandated, parents can feel obliged to attend despite having mixed feelings about therapy. Trying to clarify some of this in the assessment session is helpful. Talking openly about what prompted the referral and how everyone views the problem is important.

Engaging both the parents and the child is a challenge for therapists, as children and parents often view the problem differently. While parents may be motivated to work on the problem, children may not be. It is easy for the parents' perspective to overshadow the child's in that first session; however, ensuring that children feel important and understood is essential to engaging them. Therapists often find that early in their careers they tend to focus too much on parents to the exclusion of the children or, alternatively, that they engage with the children and find it more difficult to work with parents. It is good to be aware of your own tendencies and to have some understanding of why this occurs for you. We watched a striking example of this when a young therapist was completing an assessment in front of a one-way screen. The therapist was agreeing with the child's father, who was saying that he felt that the child was no longer depressed and did not need to attend further sessions. The child sat silently beside her father with tears rolling down her face and, while this was painfully obvious to everyone behind the screen, it went unnoticed by the therapist and the father. It was possible to use the perspective provided by the screen to reflect on what we had noticed about the child's experience of the session and the family engaged in subsequent assessment and intervention with good results. It was a good reminder of the need to monitor the reactions of all in the room.

First sessions are like any initial social encounter in that they can shape the success or otherwise of the relationship. When children and parents experience the first session as positive they are more likely to want to come back. For parents, it is crucial that they feel they are working in partnership with the therapist, do not feel blamed or criticized, and feel like the situation can improve. Reflecting on their strengths or commenting on what they have done well often helps. Sometimes, when a family has had a particularly difficult time, it can be enough to praise them for their ability to get help and to reassure them that you will be able to assist them or to find someone else who can. For children, it is important that they have had a chance to voice their views if they choose to do so and that they have felt understood by the therapist. They need to feel like they have some choices about therapy. Most of all, the first session needs to be fun for children. Rather than expecting that children sit quietly and discuss the problem like adults it is important that you engage them with play and drawings.

Children are part of a system

Another significant difference about child work is that children are very much embedded in a system. They are part of a family, a preschool or school, a broader community, and a culture. As a therapist working with children it is important that we work with this system. We work to engage parents at the time of the referral and throughout the therapy process. Consideration of the child's attachment to their parents and their relationships with siblings as well as extended family is an important aspect of our assessment. Having an awareness of the family's strengths and weaknesses informs our understanding of the child's current difficulties and shapes our work with the family.

We also need to have a clear understanding of what is happening for a child at childcare, preschool or school. Sometimes this will involve little more than an initial questionnaire or a phone call to the teacher. For children who are having significant difficulty in the classroom environment, we work closely with the class teacher and school staff.

Needing to work with the system around the child adds a layer of complexity and even experienced therapists can find it difficult to factor this into their work. Thinking carefully about the context in which you work and how you can effectively support the system around the child is crucial. For example, if you work in a school context you may like to ask that parents attend every third session and email them some brief notes after each session.

If you work in private practice you will need to talk with families about how you liaise with the child's teacher and whether there are additional fees that you charge for doing so. We've spoken with therapists who are reluctant to work with children because of the strong influence of parents, families, and schools. However, it is because of this strong influence that working with the family and school, as well as with the child, can be so powerful in creating positive change. It is an aspect of child work that we find rewarding, and well worth the time and effort.

The broader context in which children are growing up also bears mentioning. This varies across cultures and also across time. Consider, for example, how your childhood differs from that of your children or the children you work with. One clear example is the greater access to technology that children now have and the unprecedented immediacy of information. This was highlighted for one of us recently when a nine-year-old client explained that they had looked us up online! Thinking more broadly about the implications of such technology raises some other interesting questions. What does it mean to grow up in a world where information is so quickly available? What is the role of grandparents and other elders within the community when information is so widely available? Does technology help families to maintain closer connections with extended family who are living far away?

Another factor is that children today seem to have busier schedules, and are growing up in a culture in which they have less free play time. Gray (2011) documents the decline of free play over the past 50 years, noting that the incidence of mental health difficulties has increased over this period. While this data does not support a causal link, Gray makes a convincing argument that free play promotes good mental health.

Keeping these factors in mind and helping families to negotiate these challenges is an important aspect of therapy. For example, families may identify that feeling overcommitted contributes to some of the difficulties they are experiencing. Exploring how they can free up some family time may be a helpful intervention. It is important, however, not to assume that you understand an individual family's experience or perspective. Taking the time to learn about a family's challenges as well as their strengths and resources is essential.

Children are still developing

One of the wonderful things about working with children is that we never find it hard to maintain hope. Children are constantly developing and changing and are full of the possibility of change and growth. It is this ongoing development, however, that presents some challenges for us as therapists. Children are not adults and, if it is to be successful, our therapeutic approach needs to be modified significantly. Indeed working with children requires a very different way of thinking about difficulties and a markedly different approach to facilitating sessions. Children need therapy that fits with their cognitive, social and emotional development and that includes their family.

The way in which we present therapy to children needs to differ from the talk-based therapy we use with adults. Ronen (1997) wrote that working with children requires "continuous adjustments, adaptations, and translations for children at different developmental stages" (p.xviii). Therapists who work with children are, by necessity, creative; adapting the way in which they present therapeutic concepts in order to make these meaningful and understandable. Stallard (2013) suggests building in metaphor and using art, play and games to explain the core concepts of CBT. We likewise use playful and creative activities to introduce therapeutic concepts to children in a way that they can understand and use. Indeed, we argue that play is essential to making therapy developmentally appropriate for children, and we discuss this in detail in Chapter 3.

Just how different child work is became apparent to us recently when one of the therapists we supervise attended our workshop. The therapist had worked for around five years with both adults and children and decided to give up child work following the workshop. Given that we endeavor to promote working with children and like therapists to leave our workshops feeling re-energized and inspired, we were initially quite dismayed. However, the therapist felt that the workshop had helped her to understand how differently she needed to work with children. She felt she would need to think more about the way she presented therapy, organize some more craft materials and spend more time working with schools. She was also mindful that the physical space in which she was working was not well set up for children. The decision to focus on adults was a positive one for her.

Part of the reason that intervening with children is so important is precisely because they *are* still developing. Emotional difficulties can impact upon the process of development and place children at risk for developing other difficulties. For example, when a child is unable to attend school as a result of their emotional difficulties we try to get them back to school as soon as possible to limit the impact on their academic and social development.

CHAPTER 2

The Importance of Assessment

In this chapter we explore ideas relating to assessment and its importance in planning therapy for children and families.

Child and family assessment

Much of our training focused on assessment and it is in hindsight that we realized the true value of this. Having a good understanding of the problem and being able to understand what is occurring for the child and to put this in the context of the family is an essential skill. While assessment is, and should always be, ongoing, the majority of it is undertaken in the first few sessions. The areas that you should gain an understanding of during these early sessions are outlined in the box below.

FAMILY AND CHILD ASSESSMENT

What the problem is (including symptoms, frequency, duration, and triggers).

When it started.

Who it affects.

What makes it better or worse.

What the child's strengths are.

What they are interested in.

What the child finds hard.

What their early development was like.

What their early attachments were like.

Who is in the family.

How the child relates to each of the family members.

How the family works together.

Whether the child has had any previous problems.

Whether anyone else in the family has had a similar problem.

What other supports the family have (extended family, friends, etc.).

How the child is doing at childcare/preschool/school.

What has helped or not helped in the past.

What the child and family's expectations of therapy are.

What the child/family would like to change.

Initial assessment sessions

Our initial sessions vary in regard to who attends, as this depends on the family, their situation and their preferences. We tend to discuss this on the phone with parents when setting up the initial appointment. We welcome all family members to the initial session, though in practice it is often a subset of the family who attend, typically the referred child and a parent. Depending on your setting and the kinds of children you see, you may be able to offer a longer first session, providing some time with the family, some with the parents, and some with the child on their own if they are older. Occasionally parents will request that they attend the first session without their child so that they can provide important background information, some of which they may be reluctant for the child to hear.

A parent interview provides an opportunity for obtaining much of the information needed at assessment. Hearing the parents' story, getting a picture of what the child's life is like, and beginning to think about how therapy might proceed are all important aspects of the parent interview. Carr (2016) provides a good summary of how to conduct a parent interview for anyone who feels this was not well covered in their training. The parent interview also provides a space in which to begin understanding relationships within the family, including early attachments. Cassidy and Shaver's (2016) handbook is a useful resource for anyone wanting to learn more about attachment.

Sometimes asking all of the family to attend the first session works well in regard to engaging all family members in the therapeutic process, gaining an understanding of family relationships through observations, and gathering assessment information. It is important for everyone to understand the purpose of the family session, which at this stage is usually for the therapist to get to know the family and hear a little about the problem. Typically, assessment considers whether there is too great a distance or excessive closeness between family members, whether there is an ability to work through conflict and solve problems, whether the organization within the family is structured yet flexible enough to manage change, whether parents are able to work as a team, whether difficulties in the broader family causes disruption and whether members are able to communicate and respond appropriately to the feelings of others (see Lask 1987). Engaging the whole family in a hands-on activity, such as a game or drawing a genogram together, is helpful. In Chapter 4 we provide some practical ideas for family sessions, some of which may be relevant for this initial session.

Using play in the assessment phase

The core proposition of this book is that therapy needs to be presented through play in order to be appropriate for children. Similarly, child assessment should involve alternative ways in which the child can express their experience rather than relying on questions and answers. Playful, hands-on activities are important in engaging children and helping them to feel comfortable. This might include drawing, playing with puppets, or molding with clay.

Play activities can provide a focus, enabling the child to feel more comfortable communicating. Research has demonstrated that children talk more while they are drawing, providing more detail than they do when talking alone (for example, see Macleod, Gross and Hayne 2013; Woolford *et al.* 2015). Clinically, we often find that using drawing and toys during our assessment helps children to feel more relaxed, with the result that they seem more open to talking about topics that might otherwise be difficult to discuss.

Play provides a means for children to communicate about their experience and for therapists to gain an understanding of the child's perspective. We use projective techniques during our assessments, such as free play and asking the child what they would choose if granted three wishes. We also have the child complete some drawings, including a family drawing and others, such as drawing a good and bad dream or a picture of themselves at school. We interpret what children generate and integrate this with our other assessment findings. For example, a ten-year-old girl who was asked to draw her family drew each member engaged in their own activity. She labeled the picture, indicating that both her parents were working. This provided the therapist with her perspective on her family and fitted with the busy life her parents described in the parent interview. It also helped the therapist hypothesize that some of her behavioral difficulties might be accidentally rewarded with attention from her parents.

Geldard, Geldard and Yin Foo (2013) provide a detailed discussion about using drawing as well as other media, such as painting, collage, construction, miniature animals, soft toys, puppets, pretend play and clay, to assist children in expressing their experience either directly or indirectly through projective techniques. Malchiodi (1998) is a helpful reference for anyone who would like further information on drawing. Interpretation of a child's play always needs to be undertaken cautiously, with the therapist carefully understanding this in the context of all of the other assessment information collected.

The way in which a child plays also provides a lot of useful assessment information. For example, children may move quickly from one activity to another or may be cautious and careful in their approach. They may involve therapists in their play or they may prefer to play alone. These observations often help to better understand a child and develop a good formulation.

Monitoring

Monitoring is a typical part of many child therapy programs and it serves an important role, providing a baseline and helping to identify triggers and patterns. Typically parents are asked to identify what happened before the incident, describe the incident and then note what happened after. More formally in behavioral analysis these are referred to as ABC Charts which stands for Antecedent, Behavior and Consequence Charts. Carr (2016) provides a number of examples of monitoring charts for a broad range of problems that can readily be adapted.

While this sort of monitoring is very informative, it is also very labor intensive. Consider, for example, a mother of three with a child who is having five to six angry outbursts a day. It is unlikely that this mother would have the ability to record this information; however, it is likely that asking her to do so would result in her feeling unsupported. Having this occur early in therapy can impact negatively on engagement and may even mean that a family chooses not to continue.

During the assessment phase we try to have parents describe some recent instances of behavior, from which we endeavor to identify some patterns. We ask the parent to provide a detailed description of the behavior, asking that they describe it to us as though they were watching a video of it that we were unable to see. This often gives us a good sense of the behavior so that we can begin with some simple intervention strategies. We then work with parents to make monitoring manageable for them, being guided by them about what is feasible. Sometimes this means that we do not ask parents to do any monitoring, particularly if they are feeling very overwhelmed.

When we do ask parents to do some monitoring we choose something simple. We might ask, for example, that parents write down one incident from each day once the children are asleep or we might ask that they put a tick on the calendar when a behavior occurs, providing a frequency tally. Alternatively we might try having them notice and record times when their child has stayed calm or managed well. Older children can sometimes do some monitoring of their own and may like to make a "brave book," recording moments when they were able to cope despite being worried. Other examples include noting how they are feeling and what they are thinking when they get a headache, or simply circling a feeling face to indicate how they felt.

Information from preschools and schools

Children spend a large portion of their life at childcare, preschool/kindergarten or school and it is important to know what their life there is like. We like to have a sense of how a child is functioning academically, how they are behaving in the classroom, what their friendships are like and any social or emotional difficulties they might be experiencing at their preschool or school. Typically we like to do this during the assessment phase. While it is always helpful to talk to teachers over the phone, time constraints do not always make this manageable. As such, we tend to ask parents to take a questionnaire to the class teacher and let them know that their child is seeing us. We find that the act of taking the questionnaire and talking about coming to therapy with their child's teacher is helpful. Parents will sometimes come to the next session with a clearer understanding of how their child is functioning at school or with a new sense of support. Teachers will sometimes follow up by phoning us and we will make contact with a phone call or suggest a meeting if there are significant issues in that environment. The questionnaire we use is a simple and quick one for teachers and is shown in the box below.

TEACHER QUESTIONNAIRE

Please describe the child's academic progress across all areas (for school-aged children).

Please describe the child's social skills and friendships.

What do you see as the child's strengths?

Please list any concerns you have about the child.

Please describe any strategies you have tried to help the child and indicate whether or not these have been successful.

Is the child currently receiving any additional support?

Please feel free to add further comments or to contact us if you would like further discussion.

Formulation and its importance in treatment planning

Formulation is an essential skill in understanding the factors influencing a child's emotional difficulties. A formulation is a theory about why this child has developed these presenting problems and why they have developed at this particular point in time or why the family has chosen to seek help now. A child's strengths, as well as a family's resources, are also considered as part of a formulation, as these may be utilized in therapy. A common model of formulation that we find helpful incorporates the four Ps, that is:

- predisposing factors which place children at risk for developing psychological problems

- precipitating factors which trigger the onset or marked worsening of the difficulties

- perpetuating factors which serve to maintain the difficulties

- protective factors which prevent further exacerbation of the problems and have positive implications for prognosis.

This approach is well described by Carr (2016), who integrates this four Ps model with the biopsychosocial approach by sub-classifying these factors into personal or contextual domains. Carr (2016) identifies biological and psychological characteristics of the child as personal factors, and features of the child's psychosocial environment, such as family, school, peer group and involved treatment agencies, as contextual factors. These represent many varied factors that are important both in understanding the development and maintenance of a child's emotional difficulties, and in providing appropriate therapeutic interventions. The biopsychosocial model and the four Ps approach to formulation are also well described by Henderson and Martin (2007).

A thorough assessment and formulation is a prerequisite to appropriate treatment planning and engaging in therapy. The aim of this book is not to provide an introduction for assessment. We would, however, emphasize how crucial assessment is and how much it informs the work that we do. Our formulation guides our treatment plan, which in turn guides the interventions and activities we choose. Often our treatment plans are broader than the types of therapeutic interventions we present in this book. For example, they may involve referrals elsewhere to address other factors impacting on the child, such as parental mental health concerns or marital conflict, protective or environmental concerns, or medical issues. Sometimes these other factors mean that the child or family are not able to engage in the types of activities we present in this book when we first see them. Most disciplines have good training in assessment. However, if it would be helpful for you to review your assessment process then please consider reading the comprehensive information on clinical assessment of children provided by Carr (2016) or by Bostic and King (2007).

As noted previously, assessment continues throughout therapy, with the therapist monitoring the problem and continually learning about the child and family. Similarly, therapy begins from our initial contact with the family and assessment should be therapeutic. Often this is about collating all of the relevant information and helping the family to better understand the problem or to see it from a different perspective.

The value of diagnosis

Diagnoses can be valuable, helping a family to understand a child's difficulties and guiding intervention. A diagnosis does not, however, take into account individual child and family factors the way a formulation does. A diagnosis describes a set of symptoms and does not explain why these arose or are maintained. A good formulation guides therapy in a way that diagnoses may not. For example, if your formulation is that a child's difficulties are exacerbated by inconsistent parent management strategies this will clearly shape your work with the child's family.

It is also important to note that many diagnoses share some core difficulties, which may account for the high rate of comorbidity we see. It makes sense to identify core difficulties or functional impairments that can be addressed in therapy and clinically it is common practice to do so. There is also some evidence to support this approach. Ewing *et al.* (2015) explored the efficacy of broad-based CBT, that is CBT that is not tailored to a specific anxiety disorder but rather tries to address the core features that are present across disorders. The majority of the studies included in this meta-analysis consisted of children aged 7–14 years, with only a small number including younger children. Ewing *et al.* (2015) concluded that this approach was effective for the age group studied.

Hence, while we would certainly encourage you to diagnose appropriately, we believe that putting these diagnoses in context is essential both to understanding the problem in a meaningful way and to planning a practical approach to therapy.

CHAPTER 3

Purposeful and Playful Therapy

This chapter focuses on developing therapy goals and plans with families to ensure a collaborative and purposeful approach. We then explore the value of having a playful approach to therapy and some considerations around the use of play and language in practice.

Purposeful therapy

Therapy that is purposeful begins with the family and the therapist having a shared understanding of the problem. From a shared understanding, shared goals can be developed and therapy sessions can be planned.

Sharing a formulation

Feedback following an assessment helps the family to understand the problem and this, in and of itself, is often therapeutic. Sharing a formulation, however, requires skill and practice. Having a working formulation prepared is essential to doing this well and, particularly for newer therapists, this generally means having a written formulation. From there the therapist decides what aspects are most important to share with whom. For example, a therapist might identify one key predisposing factor and two perpetuating factors to share with the parents. Using simple language and linking the formulation with the assessment information is generally a helpful way to proceed. For example, you might talk with parents about how their child always seems to have been a little anxious, right from being a baby who needed to be held a lot. You might then go on to talk about how it seems like their child has avoided things that make her worried and that they as parents have tended to accommodate her anxiety by engaging in lots of safety behaviors.

It is often also appropriate to share a part of the formulation with the child. This might be as simple as talking with them about how their negative thoughts and belief that they won't be able to cope gets in the way of them trying new things and having fun.

Providing children and families with an opportunity to understand how you have made sense of the problem and to share their own ideas about this places everyone in a good position to begin thinking about goals for therapy. This conversation is often not lengthy;

however, we do find that it is something that we refer back to as therapy proceeds. In some situations, though, the conversation might be more complex and it might be appropriate to allocate a parent session to this.

Goal-setting

Having developed a shared understanding leads to the development of shared goals. Asking about what the family and the child would like to be different is often helpful. It is also appropriate for the therapist to suggest some goals, checking whether these suit the family. Often adopting a solution-focused approach is helpful. Questions like "How will we know that what we are doing is working?" or "How will things be different if our sessions together work?" are thought-provoking and useful when setting goals with families. Milner and Bateman (2011) provide a helpful introduction to using a solution-focused approach for those who would like to explore this further.

We write down the goals and find this is a good way of remaining focused. This is particularly true with families with multiple challenges where you can feel like there is a new problem each session. Of course we still endeavor to be responsive to families and do not rigidly adhere to our treatment goals; rather we use these as a guide, renegotiating these as therapy progresses.

Planning therapy

In our experience most children who attend for therapy are seen for short-term intervention. Services are often time-limited and funding is often tied to therapy being goal-focused. Rather than seeing children indefinitely we try to work in targeted blocks of therapy. Ceasing therapy provides an opportunity for families to consolidate what they have covered and enables us to assess whether the therapeutic work has resulted in some improvements. It provides the family with an opportunity to try managing on their own, reducing any dependence on the therapist and helping them to feel more confident about managing future challenges without support. Not attending therapy can also allow the child to spend more time with their family and friends, engaged in play and fun activities, which are essential for development.

Sometimes for children with long-standing difficulties, such as significant medical problems or developmental disabilities, having less frequent (monthly or bimonthly) therapy sessions works well. In these instances parents can implement the strategies suggested in the interim and the child has greater opportunities for practicing a newly learnt skill before returning to see the therapist. The latter is important given that many children with developmental disabilities require more repetition to learn new concepts than typically developing children.

Maintaining a goal-focused approach therefore seems sensible. Goals should be developed on the basis of your assessment of the child in collaboration with the family. The therapeutic activities you use in sessions need to be clearly linked to these goals and to your treatment plan. While this sounds simple in practice it can be easy to lose sight of your goals or to adopt the family's goals even if they don't fit with your clinical assessment. For these reasons we strongly recommend having a written formulation and treatment plan.

Playful therapy

Therapy with children needs to be playful and to use developmentally appropriate language. Many therapies rely heavily on language; however, a child's language skills are continuously developing and many of the concepts in CBT, such as cognitive distortions, are difficult for them to understand. Similarly, some of the concepts may not be relevant to children. For example, children are still developing their values and would find it difficult to talk about core beliefs. Introducing these concepts in play, however, enables the child to experience this in a hands-on way, to discover what it is you are trying to show them, and helps them to integrate this understanding. For example, an anxious child who takes the role of a worried puppet has an excellent opportunity to voice their unhelpful thoughts and try out some new strategies for managing their worries.

The importance of play

Play has long been recognized as a child's main form of communication and is therefore essential to engaging young children in therapy. Piaget's work, which positions children as learning through doing, experimenting and discovering was influential in this regard (Schaffer 2004). Sosinsky, Gilliam and Mayes (2007) also note the importance of learning how to use play therapeutically and as a means of communicating if working with young children. Indeed play itself is often viewed as integral to development. For example, Perry, Hogan and Marlin (2000) write that "Play, more than any other activity, fuels healthy development of children" (p.9). Play develops creativity, teamwork and cooperation, the ability to negotiate and compromise, and to follow rules and directions. Play also helps children learn self-reliance, self-expression, self-control, empathy, social interaction and problem solving (Perry *et al.* 2000). Gray (2011) also contends that play helps children to learn to regulate their emotions. Perhaps most importantly, though, play is fun.

While older primary school-aged children may be happy to sit and talk about difficulties, younger children tend to be best engaged with toys and other hands-on materials. For example, young children may communicate with us about their relationships through pretend play with dolls or figurines, or about their experiences with illness and medical procedures through pretend play with a toy doctor's kit.

Play is well suited to therapy with children. For example, consider Vygotsky's comment that "In play a child always behaves beyond his average age, above his daily behavior; in play it is as though he were a head taller than himself" (Vygotsky 1966, p.16). That is, play situations create a zone of proximal development, allowing the child to explore the space between what they can do independently and what they can do with assistance. At a practical level this means that through play the therapist enables the child to develop a greater level of understanding of their difficulties and enables exploration of alternatives. Many children who come to therapy are stuck in unhelpful patterns of behavior. Play within the therapy room can provide a safe space for them to explore alternatives. For example, a child may use toys to act out a situation they are struggling with at school. Similarly, by using play with puppets, and taking on different characters, children are able to experiment with different perspectives and practice different behavioral options in relevant situations. Our activity *Which animal?* provides a detailed example of using toy animals in this way, while *Rocket chair* provides a playful context to explore alternatives without toys. Older children may similarly explore different alternatives in a playful way by taking on characters in a "movie," complete with dramatic acting and a movie clapper for effect.

Marc Bekoff, a well-known American biologist, commented on the value of play in mammals, describing it as "training for the unexpected" (Špinka, Newberry and Bekoff 2001). We find this helpful when thinking about children and this element of play is also useful in therapy. Children can, for example, use doll play to anticipate some of what might happen when they commence school and explore how they might respond.

A final point that is important to consider about play is its role with parents. Erikson (2009, original work published 1950) wrote that "the playing adult steps sideward into another reality" (p.222) and it is this aspect of play that is often most helpful with parents. Like their children, many parents who come to therapy are stuck in unhelpful patterns of responding and a playful approach can allow them to see things from a different perspective and try alternative responses. For example, parents might develop an understanding of the way in which anxiety is transmitted between family members using our activity *Feelings in our family*. This may help them be more mindful of the pattern when it occurs, allowing them to respond differently. Play also allows parents to connect with their children in a positive way. Many families who come to therapy are locked in negative patterns of interacting and being able to engage in a positive manner is often very helpful.

Many young children with mental health difficulties also have language, processing, social and motor difficulties. These children are better able to understand concepts when these are presented in a hands-on manner, with visual support and opportunities for repetition. Using play in therapy helps to make it accessible to children with language difficulties and is essential with this group. We discuss special considerations for working with children with language and learning difficulties further in Chapter 5.

The activities outlined in this book are based on ideas and concepts that form the basis of well-established therapies, namely CBT, ACT, narrative therapy and family therapy. Play is utilized in these activities to explain these concepts to children in a simpler and more meaningful manner. This approach differs from non-directive play therapy where the focus is on the relationship between the therapist and the child, and the therapist allows the child to explore the toys and activities, interpreting their play as a product of their inner world. While these approaches are clearly valuable we find that our work with children tends to be short-term and the sorts of problems they present with are well suited to a goal-focused approach.

Using play in practice

Some therapists are naturally playful and readily integrate toys and activities into their sessions with children. Others find this more challenging. Sometimes the challenge comes from having worked more with adults or having limited experience with children. Other times therapists express feelings of embarrassment and uncertainty. Reflecting on your own tendencies is important as is being open to developing a more playful approach. We often talk in our workshops about how some therapists will feel comfortable with some of the activities while others won't. *Rocket chair* is an example of an activity that relies on a lot of imagination and role play and many of the participants in our workshop comment that they would lack the confidence to implement this. Knowing what you feel comfortable with and which activities don't suit you is important. We would encourage you to choose activities that suit your client and that you feel capable of administering.

As with therapists, parents will also vary in their capacity for play. Explaining to parents early on why you have a playful approach to therapy is important. It is also important to acknowledge that some parents find it harder to play than others and to talk about this openly.

Language in therapy

The majority of psychological therapies (such as CBT, ACT and narrative therapy) are heavily language based. Children are continually developing their ability to comprehend and use language and cannot understand concepts in the same way as adults. Using play in therapy helps children to grasp important concepts, as does using developmentally appropriate language. In addition, using developmentally appropriate language helps them to integrate these ideas into their daily life.

Play has an important role in helping children to comprehend concepts as it helps them to experience these concepts in a meaningful way. For example, while a child might find it hard to appreciate the concept of how helpful thoughts can be useful when they are worried or sad our activity *Kick-back soccer* makes this real for them. This activity is a simple way of providing children with a direct experience of the way in which helpful thoughts can be used to counter unhelpful ones.

Keeping your language simple is important when working with children. For example, while we would never use the term "cognitive distortion" with children, our *Colored glasses* activity helps them to understand that sometimes they can view situations in a negative light and enables them to see that there are alternative interpretations.

Having a good sense of typical language development in children is essential to being able to use developmentally appropriately language in therapy. Arranging for an assessment with a speech pathologist (speech and language therapist) is important should you have any concerns about a child's language development.

A final point about language is that it is important to tune in to the language that the child and family use and adopt that in your work with them. If a child refers to their angry outbursts as "explosions" that is the terminology that is most helpful to adopt. As described previously, we often encourage the family to "name" their problem during the assessment phase. Doing so is often very helpful and the name chosen by the family tends to persist throughout therapy.

CHAPTER 4

Working with Families, Preschools and Schools

Working with children necessarily involves working with parents, families and educational settings, such as school, preschool and childcare. The sections below provide some practical considerations on doing so.

Working with parents and families

Working closely with parents and families is unique to working with children and brings further layers of complexity. Managing the needs of a child as well as those of parents and siblings can often seem overwhelming to new therapists and even as experienced therapists we still find this challenging at times. Working with parents and families, however, also provides lots of wonderful possibilities and valuable resources to assist with change. What follows below are some guidelines about working with parents and families, along with some practical suggestions for doing so.

Working with parents

Children are embedded in families and working with them requires that you work with their parents as well. All of the activities we outline in the second part of the book can be completed with parents in the room or shared with parents later if you are seeing an older child. Indeed this is the way we would encourage you to work.

Typically, in addition to engaging parents actively in the work that we do with their children, we are also engaged in parent work. By parent work we mean that we allocate some time to working directly with parents around how they interact with and support their child to enable better outcomes for the child. We work from an assumption that every parent is doing the best that they can in parenting, with the knowledge, skills and resources that they have at the time. Parents can easily feel judged or blamed by professionals, and many are experiencing self-doubts, guilt or even a sense of failure in regard to parenting by the time they come to see us. These factors can impact on how they respond to their child, and how they engage in parent work. We encourage parents to be honest about their own feelings, and we empathize with the worry or frustration that they may experience in challenging situations with their children.

One key aspect of therapy when working with parents is how they respond to their child's emotions. Parents play a central role in helping children learn to regulate their emotions. They model emotions every day and provide children with examples of how to react to emotions—both their own and those of others. Some parents focus on their child's external behavior, and benefit from assistance in recognizing the emotions that underlie that behavior. For example, a child may be engaging in aggressive or defiant behavior as a result of underlying anxiety about a situation. In this context we also need to consider the parent-child attachment relationship. Helping parents to be attuned and responsive to their child's needs for safety, security, comfort and physical care may be a focus of therapy. Some parents enjoy reading about the importance of attachment and we often recommend *Parenting from the Inside Out* by Siegel and Hartzell (2014), which is included in the reference list.

Our approach is to support parents in using the emotion coaching concept proposed by Gottman and colleagues when their child is experiencing strong feelings (Gottman, Katz and Hooven 1997). This involves responding to a child's emotions with empathy and acceptance, and supporting the child to understand and regulate their feelings before assisting them to problem solve. A central component to this approach is recognizing and labelling the child's emotion—coined "name it to tame it" by Siegel and Bryson (2012). This may be as simple as the parent reflecting the child's feelings in words, for example, "you feel worried/sad/angry because…" In this way, we are encouraging parents to acknowledge and validate their child's emotions. We encourage parents to promote the notion that all emotions are okay, the child can cope with their emotions and that parents can support them. Research findings have provided support to the idea that the use of emotion coaching by parents, including emotion labeling and exploration, is likely to assist in improving the child's emotional and social competence and behavior (Eisenberg, Cumberland and Spinrad 1998; Havighurst *et al.* 2010, 2013).

Sometimes parents need support in setting limits on their child's behavior. We encourage parents to employ discipline when needed, and discuss positive strategies to do so. However, it is helpful to distinguish disciplinable behavior from the child's emotions, to prevent the child from learning that their emotions are bad, naughty or unacceptable. For example, we may help a parent consider the idea that it is okay for their child to feel angry and to express this, though it is not okay for their child to hit others. Similarly, it is okay for a child to feel nervous about going to school, and to have their anxiety acknowledged, but they do still need to go.

Sometimes the most helpful parent work we can do is to assist the parent in understanding a child's developmental stage. This may involve exploring whether expectations are age-appropriate, or normalizing a child's behavior or emotional responses. In Chapter 5 we will be exploring childhood development in further detail. The parenting books by Hawtin (2013) or Faber and Mazlish (2012) may be helpful for therapists or parents who are interested in further reading about parenting strategies or approaches.

The research on involving parents in child therapy is somewhat limited and it is an area that requires further work. While there is a general recognition that involving parents is important, standardized programs vary in the manner in which they do so. Manassis *et al.* (2014) completed a meta-analysis of parent involvement in CBT with anxious children and adolescents. CBT was found to be effective with or without parent involvement; however, the results suggest that parent involvement may support the maintenance of treatment gains. Reynolds *et al.* (2012) found that parent involvement did *not* relate to better outcomes in a meta-analysis of CBT and behavior therapy for childhood anxiety. There are many reasons why parental involvement may not be demonstrated to positively influence therapy, including methodological differences and the reliance on child measures to reflect therapeutic gains, rather than consideration of changes in parenting practices or family functioning (for discussion see Breinholst *et al.* 2012). Clinically, our experience is that actively involving parents assists children to make therapeutic gains in the short term and to maintain these in the longer term.

Family sessions

The reality for busy families is that attending sessions together is often a challenge. In practice, we spend many sessions working with a subset of the family, typically the child who is being brought for therapy and one of their parents. There are times, however, when having a session with all family members is particularly helpful. Family sessions provide a valuable opportunity to observe first hand the way in which family members relate to each other. They also provide a chance to have family members understand and better appreciate each other's perspectives.

In practice, managing family sessions can be challenging. Keeping children engaged can be hard, particularly when their ages and interests differ. Ensuring that everyone is heard and that parents and children can be involved together in the same activity and discussion is important. Often the challenges that bring families to therapy play out in family sessions. Parents may be overly critical of their children or the children may be uncontained and climb all over each other and their parents. Indeed, one of us recalls working with a very complex family early in our career. Both parents had significant mental health issues and the father's depression was severe enough that he rarely left the house. Each of the five children had emotional and behavioral difficulties and when they attended with their mother they were extremely active, sitting on top of each other and their mother despite being of an age where children can reasonably be expected to sit in their own chairs. When enlisting the help of a colleague in engaging the family in therapy the goal was simply to have them each sit in their own chairs! The lack of boundaries within the family and the dynamic of engaging their mother through inappropriate behavior was apparent within sessions which is why being able to sit, talk and listen to each other in sessions became our first goal.

One of the most useful elements of family sessions is being able to gently reflect the patterns you observe and help the family to understand these. In the case of the family described above, this meant reflecting on how difficult it was to hear each of the family members. These patterns were explored more fully in a parent session with the mother alone. Another important aspect of family sessions is that they provide an opportunity to give voice to anyone who might go unheard. You can, for example, wonder about what someone who has been quiet during the session, or even someone who is not present, might think.

In terms of timing, sometimes asking all of the family to come in for the initial session works well, as discussed earlier in regard to assessment. A family session midway through therapy can also be timely, providing an opportunity to address any issues that have arisen in therapy and develop a plan that assists the family to move forward. Similarly, a family session towards the end of therapy enables the family to reflect on what they have achieved, both as individuals and as a family, as well as identify any future challenges and strategies that might help them to manage these better.

Practical ideas for family sessions

In our experience family sessions work best when everyone understands the purpose of the session. If the session is an initial session and you have not met the child and the family before, the purpose is usually to get to know the family and hear a little about the problem. Once therapy has commenced the purpose will depend on the issues you have identified. For example, the purpose might be to have everyone problem solve what could be done about physical aggression between the siblings. The purpose of the session should be clear when you schedule the session and should be restated at the beginning of the session.

Clarifying what will happen during the session is also helpful. For example, you can explain that you have a game you would like to play and then they will do some drawing together. Some families benefit from having you explain some rules early in the session too, such as one person speaks at a time.

We would strongly encourage the use of hands-on materials during family sessions as these help to keep children (and parents) focused. Giving careful consideration to what activities you might use when planning the session is important, as is having prepared all of the materials you might need. Obviously this should not prevent you from being responsive and following the family's lead, using other activities and games as is appropriate.

For sessions in which you are getting to know the family you may like to have them each draw a family picture individually and then share it with everyone. This provides a good opportunity to comment on the similarities in who they draw and how they draw them and allows you to explore any differences. Drawing a genogram together is also helpful and children can be actively involved in drawing the people on a large sheet of paper while you learn about the family and hear some of the family history. Hearing some of the great stories or family legends can be helpful, as can wondering what the family motto might be. Having the family work on something together or play a game can also be a helpful way of observing the way in which they relate to each other.

Family sculpting is a technique often used by family therapists in which one member of the family arranges the remaining family members to create a living sculpture under the guidance of a therapist. The way in which family members are arranged is considered to reflect relationships and patterns within the family. Hearn and Lawrence (1981, 1985) provide an early description of this technique, along with some considerations regarding its use and some examples of how sculptures might be interpreted. The manner in which families negotiate this task as well as what they produce is often very telling and it is an active task that generally engages the whole family.

The activities in this book can all be used in family sessions; however, some focus specifically on the way in which family members relate around emotions. These include *Feelings in our family*, *What lives in your house?*, *Family feelings jump* and *Yawn game* and are easily incorporated into family sessions.

Working with preschools and schools

Children spend many hours each week at preschool or school, and their teachers are often a valuable resource in assisting children with the therapy goals. Teachers can provide a different perspective regarding the child's progress and can assist the child in generalizing therapeutic concepts from the therapy room to the educational and social environment of school.

How closely we work with a childcare setting, preschool or school depends on how much the child is experiencing difficulty there. Sometimes corresponding through a teacher questionnaire at assessment and perhaps a brief letter at the end of therapy is all of the contact that we will have. Other times we will speak periodically on the phone or email the child's teacher following each session. For some children, it is helpful to visit the childcare, preschool or school, to observe the child in the setting or to discuss management strategies together with the teaching staff and parents. Sometimes an important outcome of these meetings is helping the parents and teachers to understand the perspectives of each other and begin to work together as a team in supporting the child.

When communicating with teachers we start by summarizing our formulation and treatment plan, very briefly and simply. We ask if there is anything they would like us to consider in our work with the child and recommend one or two simple things they can do in their setting. In making recommendations we try to acknowledge how busy teachers are and choose something they can do that is manageable.

On some occasions parents will be reluctant for you to contact a child's educational setting. Generally we find this occurs either because they do not believe there are any difficulties there or because they have experienced some conflict with the teacher. In these cases we would of course respect the family's wishes; however, we would review this from time to time and leave open the possibility that we might be able to work with the teacher at a later date. For example, an 11-year-old client who came in to see one of us had a long history of bullying. His mother had found school unsupportive and the child echoed her view that the school was hopeless and did nothing. At the time of the assessment the mother did not want the therapist to contact the school. However, after a few sessions, she was able to see how her son's view of the school was exacerbating his low mood and preventing him from seeking help appropriately. This enabled her to make a new commitment to working with the school and making her son's remaining year there as positive as possible. Part of this commitment meant that she was happy for the therapist to contact the school and work with her son's teacher.

CHAPTER 5

Developmental Considerations when Working with Children

When working with children, it is important to have a thorough understanding of typical child development. In the following sections we summarize some key developmental considerations that are particularly relevant for therapy. For further information on child development, the chapter on normal development in Carr (2016) is very helpful. For a more comprehensive overview Berk's (2013) textbook is particularly useful.

Piaget's theory of cognitive development has influenced of our thinking about early childhood; however, more recent theorists have challenged aspects of his theory. For example, development is now thought of as more complex and uneven, rather than progressing in discrete stages, and research has suggested that Piaget may have underestimated the ages at which young children achieve some of the abilities he describes (see Berk 2013; Schaffer 2004). Despite these challenges, Piaget's proposition that children's thinking is qualitatively different from adults, and that children learn through active involvement—doing, experimenting, discovering—represents an important contribution to current understanding (Schaffer 2004). As therapists we need to provide opportunities for hands-on, active learning, and take into account developmental features of the child's thinking, particularly when engaging them in cognitive aspects of therapy, which we discuss further below. Those who are interested in reading some of Piaget's original work may like to look at Piaget (1962a and 1962b) for a brief summary of this theory.

Practically for therapists it is important that attention is paid to a child's individual capacity, ensuring that the cognitive demands of therapy do not exceed this capacity (Stallard 2013). The variations between individual children make it difficult to propose definitive suggestions about what is appropriate for specific age groups. In the following sections we talk about younger and older children. The comments in the younger children section will pertain to most children aged between four and six years, while those in the older children section are applicable to most children aged between 7 and 12 years. There will, of course, be times when the considerations for younger children relate to older children. This is particularly apparent when an older child has an intellectual disability or a language disorder, though there may be other circumstances in which this is also relevant. While these sections provide a broad guide, we would encourage you to think carefully about the children you work with and tailor your approach to their individual developmental level.

Younger children

The age at which children are able to engage in cognitive therapy has been an area of debate. Piaget's theory, which suggested that logical reasoning is only acquired at around seven to eight years of age, has been influential in this regard (Piaget 1962a, 1962b). Carr (2016) provides a summary of Piaget's theory, noting that children aged four to six are beginning to develop internal representations of their world and can play symbolically, use more sophisticated language, infer what others are thinking and distinguish between appearance and reality; all of which are valuable assets when working therapeutically. Young children are beginning to engage in problem solving, though they emphasize what they perceive rather than what they remember (Carr 2016). They are able to reason, though they do so intuitively, linking one particular instance to another, rather than reasoning from general principles to specific instances. Another factor to keep in mind when working with young children is that they have limitations around how much information they can process and remember (Carr 2016).

Young children and cognitive strategies

While CBT can involve complex reasoning, the cognitive demand of many of the CBT programs used with children is far more limited. This has led in more recent years to a consensus that children as young as seven years have sufficient cognitive abilities to engage in CBT (Stallard 2013). Stallard (2013) contends that younger children are also able to actively engage in CBT that has been appropriately modified to suit their developmental level. Research on children's cognitive and social development lends support to this proposition. For example, Wellman, Hollander and Schult (1996) found that even three-year-olds were able to understand thought bubbles with just the simple explanation that the bubbles show what a person is thinking. The young children were able to differentiate between the thoughts and actions or objects, and also showed understanding that different people could have different thoughts about the same situation.

Another factor that influences the use of cognitive strategies with young children is that they are still developing their capacity for inner talk; that is, the ability to articulate thoughts and understand the concept of talking to oneself. Alderson-Day and Fernyhough (2015) reviewed the relevant theory and research to find that children increasingly use inner talk during middle childhood. Younger children may instead use private speech, spoken out loud, to guide their behavior and regulate their emotions. One of us had the experience of taking our three children aged three, five and eight years roller skating for the first time and observed this. The three-year-old required lots of reassuring words, while the eight-year-old readily attempted skating without needing any reassuring words. It was, however, the five-year-old who was most interesting. He stayed close and said out loud comments like "it's okay, it's just my first time" and "practice makes perfect." While it may have looked like he was reassuring his mother (who was also wobbling on her skates), it was clear that he was using private speech spoken out loud to reassure himself.

Research findings

Much of the research supporting the efficacy of CBT with children has involved children older than about seven years. More recently, programs have been modified for younger age groups, demonstrating that CBT can be successfully adapted for use with preschool-aged children as young as four with promising results (Barrett *et al.* 2015; Hirshfeld-Becker *et al.* 2008; Pahl and Barrett 2010). Modifications have included actively involving parents, using self-instructive training rather than sophisticated cognitive restructuring (Hirshfeld-Becker *et al.* 2008) and using experiential, play-based activities (Pahl and Barrett 2010).

Hirshfeld-Becker *et al.* (2011) reviewed a small number of studies utilizing CBT with younger children (including some that included preschoolers) to find that there was promising support for the efficacy of CBT in children under eight years of age. Similarly, Grave and Blisset (2004) reviewed the literature on young children and CBT as well as developmental theory to conclude that young children "can demonstrate the cognitive capacity to benefit from creatively delivered forms of CBT" (p.417). The authors suggested that integrating cognitive, social and emotional developmental theories into CBT was important, along with the use of narrative and analogy.

This suggests that children may be able to engage in CBT from a young age if the therapist is able to structure activities in a suitable manner. Many CBT programs with children emphasize behavioral strategies, spending less time on cognitive strategies. Often the cognitive strategies that are included are limited and simplified (Stallard 2013). For example, there might be a focus on developing coping self-talk in younger children and it is reasonable to assume that if presented appropriately most children should be able to learn at least this simple strategy.

Practical implications for working with younger children

Practically this means that young children learn best through play and hands-on experiences rather than talking. Their language development is such that play remains the best format for engaging and teaching them. Preschoolers often refer to emotions in imaginative play, providing opportunities for therapeutic interventions. A preschooler's ability to play symbolically is also an asset in therapy, meaning that they can readily appreciate that worries are like butterflies or that their anger can be like a fire. Their ability to distinguish reality from fantasy means that they rarely need to be reassured about the difference between these games and metaphors and real life. They benefit from repetition and reinforcement so you may need to use a number of different activities focusing on the one skill. For example, young children who present for therapy often need to work on expressing their emotions and benefit from having a number of opportunities to do so. Working closely with parents helps in this regard too, as parents can talk with their children at home about concepts that have been introduced, providing repetition and assisting generalization by pointing out similarities between what was discussed in the therapy session and what happens in the child's day-to-day life.

Another consideration when meeting the learning needs of young children is using appropriate language and providing only a small amount of information at any one time, allowing sufficient time for the child to process and understand it. Generally with young children we aim to work on just one concept in a session. For example, we might work on the idea that feelings come and go, perhaps using the *Feeling bubbles* activity and reinforcing this with puppets, role play and drawings. Obviously we would be working simultaneously with the parents on other goals. For example, we might be asking that the parents label the child's emotions and empathize with them, that they note down any triggers and that they provide the child with some calm-down options.

In terms of social development, young children are beginning to separate from their parents and to socialize more with others, as their social world broadens to include childcare or preschool settings. This can be a challenge for many young children who present for assistance around separation anxiety. Preschoolers interact more with other adults, such as their teachers, and have greater opportunity and ability to interact with their peers. Despite their increased autonomy, most preschool children will need their parents to remain in the therapy room with them in order to allow them to feel secure.

Involving parents in therapy is essential to monitoring what is happening at home. Young children's limitations in language and egocentric tendencies can mean that they have difficulties recounting events coherently. They can find it hard to understand the perspective of others, though they are often eager to please and may say what they think the therapist wants to hear. We have certainly had the experience of having children tell us that they have not had any meltdowns since their last session only to look over and see their parents shaking their faces in shock. Having a clear understanding of what is happening at home enables us to monitor and review our progress and to adapt our approach as needed.

Perhaps most importantly, our work with young children focuses on behavioral strategies—that is, what they can *do*. We do, however, include at least a brief mention in therapy of helpful thoughts. Preschoolers are of an age where they have some concept of thoughts, though they may need to speak helpful thoughts aloud, and be prompted by parents to do so, to assist them in challenging situations. There are a number of simple helpful thoughts that apply to a range of situations, thereby avoiding some of the problems around generalization. For example, "I can do it" is a helpful thought that is appropriate for a child as he farewells his mother at preschool and as he tries his bike without training wheels for the first time. Similarly, "I can try" or "practice makes perfect" is a helpful thought that is well suited to children who are soon to enter school, as it applies to many of the challenges they will face.

Another advantage of including some helpful thoughts when working with preschoolers is that it cues parents into the importance of thoughts and their influence on emotions and behavior. This provides parents with an opportunity to model, reflect on and reinforce helpful thoughts long after therapy has ceased.

Structuring sessions with young children

Ideally parents will be present when you work with a preschool-aged child; however, you will also need some time to work with parents alone. Having time with parents allows you to ask about the child's progress and provides an opportunity for them to raise any new concerns. It also provides a crucial space for talking with parents about how they can support what the child has learnt in therapy and to discuss other parenting strategies that sit alongside your work with the child.

Often we structure sessions so that we have 30 minutes working with the parent and child and then 30 minutes to talk with parents. We find this works well as young children only have a short attention span and it is best to finish and move them onto something else if they begin to lose interest. Indeed some children can only manage 20 minutes or so. Often children at this age can be engaged in free play with toys, which allows you to talk with parents. If the child is particularly active, or if the parent or therapist feel it would be more appropriate to speak alone, then you may consider having another family member or friend take the child out of the room. Another alternative is to ask the parent to bring a portable DVD player or a tablet for the child to play on. Sometimes children will happily watch a movie with their headphones in, which helps parents feel comfortable about speaking. Scheduling a parent appointment can also be helpful at times.

Getting set up for young children

Having appropriately sized furniture and some toys in easy reach tends to make the clinic room inviting for young children. We like having some colorful cushions on the floor that can readily be stacked or toppled. If possible it is lovely to have a life-size teddy in the room and having a couple of doll houses is also ideal. The reality is, however, that many therapists work in a number of settings across their week, often using clinic rooms that are shared with others. We have been mindful of this in thinking about what we find useful for working with children and have tried to choose materials that are easily transported. Often therapists work with a range of different presenting problems and age ranges and are reluctant to spend a large amount of money on resources. For this reason we have also tried to use materials that are readily available and inexpensive. The materials we suggest you consider including in your therapy toolkit are listed in the box at the end of this section.

Much of what we use with preschoolers are craft materials. When choosing art materials we look for brands that easily wash from clothes and furniture, such as washable markers and watercolor paints. We find play-doh useful and usually have a set of tubs in a range of colors with some utensils for cutting and shaping. If you are working in a carpeted room you may like a plastic mat that you can lay out below this. A selection of puppets is also very useful with this age group though you may want to consider finger puppets if space is limited.

We find blocks useful for stacking and toppling. Wooden and plastic blocks can have pictures glued on them and are useful for activities such as *Feeling block people*. Similarly, a soft cloth ball is great for throwing around while engaging in conversation and can be used for activities such as *Kick-back soccer*. Balloons are helpful because these take little storage space and can be a good substitute for a ball, can have faces drawn on them, be used to make stress balls, or used in scaling activities described in Chapter 6.

Anything that prompts a discussion about feelings is helpful so it is worth thinking about having some emotion cards or other cards that can be used to symbolize how a child is feeling. For example, a child may choose from a range of picture cards to indicate their state of mind. Having a poster depicting various feeling faces on your wall is another way to encourage talk about feelings, as are books about feelings or toys that show feelings.

In preparing for work with young children, we often try to include activities that get them out of their seat and moving. Activities that involve throwing and jumping are great; however, sometimes even just moving from one part of the room to another is helpful in breaking up the session and maintaining a child's interest.

THERAPY MATERIALS

Chunky markers and crayons (younger children).

Pencils, thinner texta pens and gel pens or pastels (older children).

Watercolor paints.

Scissors, glue and tape.

Paper and cardboard—different types, colors and sizes.

Paper plates, bags, and cups.

Cardboard cut-outs of body or hand shapes, door hangers, crowns, blank puzzles and glasses.

Cardboard boxes and bags in different sizes, shapes and colors.

Glitter for decorating (doubles as magic dust).

Popsicle sticks, pipe cleaners, googly eyes and similar for making puppets, dolls or creatures.

Play-doh (younger children), modeling clay or air-drying clay (older children).

Balloons, bubbles and dice.

Blocks, soft ball and puppets.

Feelings visuals such as a poster or cards.

Older children

Children aged between about seven and 12 years are a great group to work with. Clearly this age range covers a broad range of developmental stages and working with a seven-year-old is vastly different to working with a 12-year-old. For the purpose of this brief introduction, however, we consider some key features of this period and their implications for therapy.

Emotionally, children in this age group have made some significant gains. Carr (2016) comments that children of this age prefer to regulate their emotions autonomously rather than involve parents as they would have done when younger. They are beginning to understand mixed emotions, and have learnt what displays of emotion are acceptable and to hide unacceptable emotions.

Socially, children begin to differentiate from their parents and develop their own views. They are increasingly aware of how they fit in. Indeed, Combrinck-Graham and Fox (2007) wrote that "the most significant emotional issues in the lives of school-aged children concern personal worth that is determined by a sense of competence and place in family, peer group, and communities" (p.271). Social demands increase with age and children who have social difficulties can find this particularly challenging. As such, it is important to understand how a child relates to their family, as well as how they function at school and in other social settings, and to work closely with parents, teachers and anyone else who might be relevant.

Older children are more independent and, once a rapport is developed, they generally like to be actively involved in therapy. They can be involved in setting goals and doing so usually makes them more invested in therapy. Although many children will not be able to see longer-term goals, they will be able to articulate something such as "not feeling worried all the time" and doing so enables them to feel more in charge of the process.

With their increasing independence, it is often helpful for older children to spend some time alone with the therapist. This provides them with a safe, private space to explore their thoughts, feelings and experiences, and can empower them to take an active role in creating change. However, involving the family, and in particular the parents, in the therapy remains crucial. Confidentiality becomes increasingly important and needs to be negotiated with the child.

Children of this age are very aware of how others perceive them so it is important that their emotions and experiences are normalized when they come to therapy. This helps them to feel less alone and can help to generate hope or optimism for overcoming their current difficulty. Letting children know that you have seen other children with similar difficulties often helps to normalize their experience, as can exploring appropriate books or websites on the topic. Sometimes we like to help children understand the prevalence of such difficulties in a simple manner, by talking about how many children in their class or school are likely to have similar difficulties.

Older children and cognitive strategies

From a cognitive perspective, Piaget noted that most older children are able to use concrete logic though they may continue to have difficulty understanding abstract or hypothetical concepts (Piaget 1962a, 1962b). Older children are beginning to develop cognitive self-regulation (Combrinck-Graham and Fox 2007). With their ability to reason logically and to manage their emotions by changing their thoughts, children are now more able to benefit from the cognitive aspects of therapy. Most older children can reflect on thoughts in therapy. They can learn about the impact of thoughts on feelings and can consider which thoughts are helpful or unhelpful. Their increased ability to reason logically also means that they can begin to engage in challenging thoughts, by looking for evidence and being a thought detective, though they often require scaffolding to do so.

Maintaining a playful approach to therapy provides older children with the support they need in order to benefit from the cognitive aspects of therapy. Stallard (2002) argues that "the challenge for the practitioner is to translate abstract concepts into simple, concrete everyday examples to which the children can relate" (p.16). Thought bubbles are an example of making an abstract concept more concrete. Metaphors are also helpful in this regard, and we make use of these in a number of our activities, such as *Big volcano* for working on anger and *Butterfly catching* for working on worries.

Older children can use their imagination to comfort themselves. For example, a nine-year-old we worked with had some separation anxiety when settling to sleep of an evening and found it was helpful to imagine that her mother was in bed beside her reading a book. Picturing this helped her to feel less anxious and enabled her to fall asleep without her mother in the room.

Interestingly, despite older children having an increased capacity for using cognitive strategies, clinically we find that they still seem to use behavioral strategies more often. We often ask children who are finishing therapy what the most helpful thing was and typically it is a simple behavioral strategy such as learning that they can walk away. As a result, we try to include a mix of cognitive and behavioral strategies, adjusting the ratio of each depending on what seems to suit the child best.

Parenting work continues to be a big focus

In keeping with this we try to have time with children and time with parents each session. We update parents on what we have worked on in the session and talk about anything that needs to happen at home before the next session. This also provides an opportunity to undertake any parent work we might be focusing on. The way in which we structure sessions tends to vary depending on where we are at in therapy. Sometimes more parent work is needed and so we might spend half the session with the child and half with the parent. At other times working with the child will be the focus so we might see the child for the majority of the session and bring the parent in for the last 15 minutes or so. Sometimes we will see a child for half an hour, spend 15 minutes with both the child and the parent, and then spend the last 15 minutes with the parent.

The most natural way we have found of sharing with parents what we are working on with children is to have them join us in the session and ask that the child show them what we have done. Children are typically happy to show their parents a picture they have drawn or a game they have played and this is an easy way to involve parents and provide feedback. It often also allows us to get a sense of what the child has taken from the activity and to reinforce what they have learnt. Another advantage of this strategy is that the child is in control of what they tell their parents about the session, thus empowering the child and avoiding some of the issues around confidentiality.

Older children are generally happy to wait in the waiting room so long as they have something to read or play with. You may want to suggest that parents bring something that their child can do while they are waiting if your waiting room is not well stocked, or you may provide the child with an appropriate book or activity. Reception staff are sometimes available to keep an eye on children in the waiting area; however, if they are not, it is important to consider whether the child is safe to wait in there.

Confidentiality

A level of confidentiality is required to build a trusting and therapeutic relationship with school-aged children. It can also ensure a safe space where children can share their worries and concerns without fearing negative consequences from others. At the same time, it is important to share information with parents to help them understand the work children are doing in therapy, how they can support this work at home, and their child's progress, as well as any other specific feedback that is likely to be helpful for the child and family. We do this in consultation with the child to protect confidentiality.

Older children need an explanation about confidentiality. Generally with children it is sufficient to say that this means that what they tell us is private but that there are some limits to this. You can then go on to explain that most parents like to know what is going on and how they can help, so you and the child can decide each session what you will let them know. The other limit that we explain to children is that if we are worried that they are unsafe we would need to tell someone in order to keep them safe.

At the end of each session, we talk quickly with the child about what they will tell their parents about the session and what it is okay for us to say. Whilst we try to stick to general ideas we find that, at times, it is helpful for us to convey something very specific that the child has expressed. In these instances we ask for consent to share this information.

Parents may feel anxious about their child speaking confidentially to a therapist and need a clear explanation about how this will work in practice—that is, how we plan to keep them involved and informed while protecting confidentiality for their child. This generally includes reassurance that they will be kept up to date with what is occurring in therapy and will be given feedback and information so that they are able to help. Parents also often find it reassuring to know they will be informed if there are any concerns about safety.

In practice we find that most children will happily share with their parents what they have discussed in sessions. Where they do want something kept private, it is often a detail that is unrelated to the main elements of the therapy. Indeed with some children we find it easier to ask whether there is anything they do not want us to share with their parents rather than discussing what we can share with them. This is often more time-effective, particularly for children who have not shown any previous concern about you communicating with their parents.

Getting set up for older children

Much of what we use with older children is similar to what we use with younger children, and our earlier list incorporates therapy materials we use with both age groups. We continue to rely heavily on craft materials with this age group. Visual supports also continue to be helpful and many of the commercially available strength cards or feelings cards help to elicit discussion.

Children of this age are often beginning to be able to sit and talk for longer. Often having something to play with assists them with this. This might be a fiddle toy, something sensory that fits comfortably in their hand that is enjoyable to play with. Choosing something that still allows the child to focus on talking to you is important. Sometimes coloring in, or playing with something simple, such as kinetic sand, provides a soothing sensory experience that the child can focus on while speaking. An activity such as this can make the discussion seem less threatening and increases the likelihood that children will speak more during sessions.

Older children also enjoy activities that get them up and out of their seats. Games that involve jumping or throwing a ball around the room are often engaging, while other children may enjoy going for a walk with the therapist. Older children are generally happy to remain at table top activities for longer and we see a number of children who particularly enjoy drawing and will happily spend the entire session on pen and paper activities. Providing a mix of more active activities and pen and paper ones is ideal for older children.

Individual differences and developmental concerns

While we have talked more generally about younger and older children there is obviously great variation between children of the same age. Having a good sense of your client's developmental level in addition to their chronological age is essential.

Children with developmental delays or disorders may present with difficulties with emotional regulation so consideration of a child's development is an important part of your assessment. This requires familiarity with typical child development as well as awareness of common developmental disorders, such as Intellectual Disability (ID) and Autism Spectrum Disorder (ASD).

ID (referred to as General Learning Disability in the United Kingdom) describes a pattern of impaired intellectual functioning, which is associated with deficits in adaptive functioning.

Impaired intellectual functioning is defined as more than two standard deviations below the mean on standardized tests of cognitive functioning, with levels of impairments ranging from mild to severe. Language disorder describes children who have significantly impaired language abilities that persist from an early age. Comprehensive assessment with a speech pathologist is essential to diagnosis of a language disorder and a referral is essential should you have any concerns about a child's language development. ASD is a developmental disorder that is characterized by social communication difficulties and repetitive behaviors. Children with ASD may also have cognitive and language impairments or may be high functioning, performing in the average range. Attention Deficit/Hyperactivity Disorder (ADHD) may be diagnosed in children who have difficulty attending to and regulating their behavior, both at home and in the classroom.

Learning difficulties are prevalent amongst children with these diagnoses and may also occur in the absence of developmental difficulties. Children with learning difficulties find school frustrating and difficult and low self-esteem often results. As with learning difficulties, language disorders have been found to be associated with poorer mental health. Howlin and Rutter (1987) were among the first to clearly articulate this pattern and more recent research has continued to find this pattern (see Beitchman, Brownlie and Bao 2014; Johnson, Beitchman and Brownlie 2010; Yew and O'Kearny 2013). Indeed, in a recent meta-analysis, Yew and O'Kearny (2013) found children with specific language impairments were twice as likely to have emotional and behavioral problems. Similarly, a number of studies have demonstrated that children with intellectual disabilities are at greater risk of developing mental health difficulties. This pattern is apparent in preschool (Dietz *et al.* 1997) as well as in school-aged children. Indeed, Chen *et al.* (2006) found that this pattern persisted into adulthood, even for those children who were assessed as having borderline intellectual functioning (that is, intellectual functioning that is well below average but not as low as to indicate ID).

Implications for therapy

A comprehensive assessment is needed to identify a child's cognitive abilities, language skills and academic achievement if any concerns regarding learning or development have been raised. Consideration of a child's memory, attention and planning, and organizational skills may also be indicated. Therapists often have an important role in completing these assessments or advocating that these are conducted through school or another service. Keeping in mind that many high-functioning children with ASD are not diagnosed until school age is also important. Referring to an appropriate clinician for an assessment, or completing an assessment yourself if this is something you do, may be indicated if the child has social difficulties or repetitive behaviors.

Helping parents to understand assessment reports and appreciate what this means for their child and how it might be contributing to some of the emotional or behavioral difficulties they are experiencing is also important. All too often we see parents who have received a complex report and are left to make sense of this without the assistance of a feedback session. Sometimes parents need help to make sense of multiple reports, integrating them in a way that helps them to better understand and support their child.

Therapy for children with learning, cognitive and language difficulties needs to be modified accordingly. We are careful about the language we use, simplifying it to a level that suits the child, and we focus even more on behavioral strategies. We avoid writing tasks with children with learning difficulties and always offer to write anything they want written in sessions. This way therapy does not become associated with another experience of failure. Similarly, if children attempt to spell a word we would accept however they spell it, explaining that therapy is not school and we know what they are writing if they express uncertainty about their spelling.

Children with learning difficulties, or cognitive or language impairments need a significant amount of support and therapists often need to work closely with schools to ensure that children are being provided with developmentally appropriate work, have some social connections and feel like part of the school community. Fostering non-academic interests and strengths is a priority, as is ensuring that children develop practical skills for day-to-day living.

Individuals with ASD have a unique set of strengths and weaknesses and it is widely accepted that CBT needs to be modified to suit this profile (Attwood and Scarpa 2013; Sofronoff, Attwood and Hinton 2005). Modifications include using visual supports, focusing on helping children to recognize emotions, increasing the time spent on concepts, using supports to maintain focus (such as a schedule or token system), decreasing session length and increasing structure within the session. Encouraging flexible thinking is recommended, as are strategies that assist with generalization, such as role play and between session rehearsal. Incorporating a child's interests is also recommended and providing alternative strategies for expressing feelings and experiences is encouraged. The use of simple metaphors to make therapeutic concepts more concrete is suggested and specific training in social skills is sometimes incorporated. Consideration of an individual's sensory needs and regular contact with parents are also important aspects to modifying therapy for use with children with ASD (Attwood and Scarpa 2013). A recent meta-analysis completed by Ung *et al.* (2015) reviewed 14 randomized controlled studies looking at the effectiveness of CBT with children and adolescents with high functioning ASD and anxiety. Participants were aged between 7 and 17 years and a moderate treatment effect was found. Therapists who work with children with high-functioning ASD are likely to find *CBT for Children and Adolescents with High Functioning Autism Spectrum Disorders* by Scarpa, Williams White and Attwood (2013) to be a helpful resource.

It is worth commenting on the role of play in therapy with children with ASD. Play helps children develop flexibility and try out new behaviors and roles. It helps children to learn to regulate their emotions and typically developing preschoolers regularly include emotions in their creative play. Therapists often feel cautious about using play in therapy with children with ASD; however, often children with ASD benefit from the use of play. In our experience the use of play with children with ASD promotes their capacity to think flexibly, to practice new behaviors or skills, and to generalize what they learn beyond the clinic room. That said, children with ASD will often need support to use play and therapists will often need to be more directive and structured in their use of play. For example, the therapist may need to carefully structure a play scenario with puppets, commenting on how it is similar to what the child experienced the other day, and providing the child with a list of the three ideas for managing anger that were generated in the previous session. This preparation may be essential to having the child role-play a strategy for managing anger, particularly early in therapy.

CHAPTER 6

Key Approaches and Helpful Ideas

There are a number of key approaches that are commonly utilized by child therapists and are included in most therapy programs. Similarly, there are a lot of helpful ideas that many therapists who work with children use. In outlining these we have made reference to activities in Part II that utilize these approaches and incorporate these ideas.

Key approaches to working with children

Recognizing and expressing feelings

Helping children identify and express their feelings is considered a core component of therapy for a range of emotional difficulties (see Jongsma, Petersman and McInnis 2014). This is common across different theoretical frameworks, including CBT and ACT as well as family therapy approaches, and is supported by research showing that greater emotional awareness and the ability to identify and verbally describe emotions predicts better emotional functioning (Ciarrochi, Heaven and Supavadeeprasit 2008; Rieffe and Rooij 2012).

Therapy tends to begin with helping children to recognize and express their feelings, as this is a prerequisite to further work. Families vary greatly in the extent to which they talk about feelings, as do children. One of us recalls watching our two-year-old son standing by the sandpit telling some friends how it made him feel to have his truck snatched away and noticing that the other children kept on digging and playing without stopping to listen to what he was saying. It was a good reminder that it is possible to talk too much about feelings!

While some children come to therapy using emotion words and being able to readily reflect on their own experiences, others find this a real challenge. It is not uncommon for children to find it difficult to articulate what they are worried, angry or sad about. Instead, they may move quickly into behavioral expressions of emotions. For example, anxiety may be expressed by clingy or avoidant behavior, complaints of physical symptoms like stomachaches, or challenging, aggressive behaviors. Often parents also feel unable to identify the triggers or emotions, and may misinterpret these behaviors as the child being naughty or sulky. The assessment is a good time to get a sense of how a child understands emotions. Asking about feelings when you are learning about the family or drawing a genogram is often helpful. For example, you can ask about who is fun to play with, who is good to talk to and the like and then ask whether there is anyone who feels sad, or anyone who gets angry a lot.

Direct discussions about feelings can be challenging for many children, and may even seem intrusive or confronting. Providing a context that is comfortable for the child to facilitate any discussion is very important. This may involve reading books about feelings, or engaging in feelings games or craft activities. In addition to the ideas below, a number of our activities in Part II may also be helpful in opening up conversations about feelings and gaining insight into a child's understanding of a range of emotions and triggers, such as *Feeling block people*, and *Pushing my buttons*. *Family feelings inventory* encourages all family members to recognize and express their emotions.

Another strategy that is commonly used by therapists to help children express their feelings is a feeling dice. You can construct a feeling dice with a child, ensuring that each face on the dice has a different feeling depicted on it, and then take turns to roll the dice, describing a time when you experienced the feeling the dice lands on. Stern (2008) describes her use of this activity and includes a blank dice proforma in her book. Dice templates are also readily available online and dice can also be made simply using cube-shaped boxes or foam cubes. A related idea is to make a feelings spinner with your client, taking turns to spin it and describe a time you felt that way. Making these with a child helps you to use their language around feelings. Emotion dominos are also simple to make with children and are utilized by some therapists to provide an opportunity to talk with children about a range of feelings.

In addition to exploring a child's understanding of emotions generally, it is often helpful to focus in on a particular emotion of relevance. When exploring worries, many therapists help children to make worry dolls, using dolly pegs with wool for clothes and a pipe-cleaner for arms, to help children articulate their worries. The legend and tradition around these tiny, hand-crafted dolls from Guatemala can be found easily online, or introduced with the delightful picture book called *Silly Billy* by Anthony Browne (2007). Our activities *Butterfly catching* and *Worry box* similarly assist with expressing worries, while *Big volcano* and *Put the fire out* focus on anger. *Straw that broke the camel's back* also focuses on exploring triggers to anger and the importance of expressing these feelings rather than holding them in.

Helping children to gain an understanding of how emotions can be related and experienced simultaneously, or how one emotion can underlie another emotion, is often a useful intervention. A number of our activities in Part II address this more complex level of emotional awareness, including *Anxious/excited coin toss*, *Feelings juggle*, *Feelings that show* and *Lift the flap on anger*.

Recognizing bodily sensations

Having the language to name feelings is important; however, recognizing emotions also relies on an awareness of the associated bodily sensations. Being aware of changing bodily sensations is an important component of ACT (see Hayes and Ciarrochi 2015) and mindfulness-based interventions (e.g. body scan meditations, such as in Willard 2010 and Etty-Leal 2010). Many

CBT programs addressing anxiety or anger difficulties in children begin with psychoeducation about the emotion, an essential component of which is the physiological changes that occur in the body (e.g. the Friends program outlined in Barrett 1999). A body picture is often used to help children map out the sensations associated with the emotion (Huebner 2005; Rapee *et al.* 2006). One of us recalls using a similar intervention when running a group about feelings for boys some years ago. We traced around the children and they drew on their body outlines to symbolize any of the physiological symptoms we described. Through this activity one child realized for the first time that he felt the need to go to the toilet when he was worried. This was a helpful revelation for both the boy and his mother and meant that she could encourage him to talk about his feelings when this pattern occurred. We consider body mapping to be a core activity in helping children manage their emotions, so although it may be familiar to many therapists, we decided it was important to include our adaptation of this activity in Part II. *Body mapping* describes how we introduce and use this intervention with children, which incorporates psychoeducation about the cognitive and physiological aspects of emotions, as well as variations that we find helpful.

Many children who come to therapy find it difficult to recognize and understand their own feelings. Many don't associate the changes that occur in their body with their emotions, and some don't even notice the bodily changes. Similarly, many are not aware of the changes in their thought patterns when experiencing different emotions. Examples usually help children to begin thinking about what they experience in their bodies, and many therapists feel comfortable sharing what they notice in their body when they are worried (e.g. that their jaw becomes tight). Books about emotions can also be helpful in providing examples and normalizing these experiences. The activity *Binoculars for looking inside* was developed to assist children in this process of recognizing and understanding their bodily sensations, as well as their thoughts. *Feelings buzzer* extends this and encourages children and families to continue to notice physical cues outside of the therapy session.

Parents often need support to cue in to a child's physical symptoms of anxiety or anger. Sometimes when they have a child who has frequent somatic symptoms, such as headaches or stomachaches, parents believe that their child is not really in pain. Helping parents to understand that the child's physical symptoms are real despite being precipitated by their emotions is important.

While for all children developing a sense of how they experience feelings in their body is important, for some children somatic difficulties will be a key element of their presentation. Understanding the relationship between anxiety and bodily sensations can help to normalize an experience that a child may otherwise find frightening or confusing. It is not uncommon for children to experience anxiety about sensations such as headaches or stomachaches if they don't understand the connection between these symptoms and their anxiety. For example, one of us saw a teenage girl with ASD who was referred for therapy only after significant medical testing had ruled out any medical cause for her stomachaches. Therapy was essential to helping her to see the connection between her anxiety and her stomachaches, thereby decreasing the anxiety she experienced about being unwell. Helping children and families to understand the connection between somatic symptoms and anxiety is often an important aspect of therapy and can be particularly important for children who lack insight into their feelings, such as those with ASD, or in families where emotions tend to be expressed through physical symptoms.

Scaling

The ability to reflect on the size of a feeling is central to many treatment programs, including most CBT programs, addressing anxiety and anger in children. Many parents comment on their child's anger coming out of nowhere and escalating from 0 to 100 in no time. Working with children, we often notice that they lack the appropriate language to describe lower levels of anger or anxiety. For example, these children will talk about being furious; however, they don't reflect on feeling annoyed or cross. Being able to identify lower levels of emotions is important because it means that children can try some calm-down strategies earlier to prevent their feelings escalating further.

We find that scaling is a central concept that we return to throughout therapy. For younger children this is often as simple as having them show us with their hands how angry or worried they felt. For older children we would tend to have them rate their feelings on a feelings thermometer or another type of scale. For example, one child who attended therapy with us and had a special interest in dinosaurs would talk about whether his feelings were brontosaurus-sized or pterodactyl-sized or something in between. With other children, we've used a computer game analogy, and talked about the different levels of the "anger game" or "worry game."

A balloon can provide an engaging visual representation of this scaling concept for children of all ages. While blowing up a balloon, we might ask a child for examples of things that make them feel angry and to show how big the balloon should go to show how angry this makes them feel. The full balloon then provides an opportunity to reflect on how the child feels when they are so angry, and gradually letting varying quantities of air out can provide a representation of how helpful particular strategies are in calming down.

A number of our activities in Part II use scaling. Sometimes scaling is the central component of the activity, such as in *Toilet paper scaling* or *Target practice*. Other activities include an element of scaling, such as *Put the fire out, Big volcano* and *Straw that broke the camel's back*. Our activity *Warning signs* similarly helps to build awareness of lower levels of emotions.

Many of you will be familiar with the concept of a "feelings thermometer" to scale fear, worries or anger, as this tends to be one of the most widely used forms of scaling and is included in a large number of CBT programs and workbooks (e.g. Rapee *et al.* 2006; Stallard 2002). Although this is not an original activity, we have chosen to share the way that we introduce and use this activity with children because we consider it a core component of CBT that can be easily varied to take into account differing interests and developmental levels of the children we see.

Relaxation, breathing and mindfulness strategies

Relaxation strategies are a central part of working with children with emotional difficulties and are included in a large number of therapy programs (e.g. Barrett 1999; Stallard 2002). We tend to think broadly about relaxation for children and find that they tend to respond best to activity-based relaxation. Learning that they can do something calming like playing LEGO® or reading a book is often helpful, particularly for younger children.

In addition, however, we often find it useful to teach some simple breathing strategies. For younger children it can be as simple as one big breath out. Young children often find breathing in a relaxing manner difficult and benefit from being able to see the impact of their breath. We find bubbles a helpful way of doing this and often use the activity that is written up in *Blow your worries away*. Paper windmills are also useful for allowing children to see the impact of their breath and to learn how to take calming breaths.

Older children are often able to engage in more traditional relaxation training, such as a progressive muscle relaxation or a relaxation script based on imagery. These relaxation scripts need to be developed specifically for children to provide appropriate language and content. There are many commercially available relaxation resources, for example, Donna B. Pincus's album *I Can Relax!* (2011). Sometimes we need to try several different approaches or scripts to find one that is appealing to the child. Many children enjoy having their own relaxation script recorded by the therapist while they practice in session.

If we are encouraging a child to practice relaxation, breathing techniques or mindfulness outside of sessions, it is important that we make it easy for them to do so, for example by providing a CD or suggesting an app. It is also important that we explain our rationale for encouraging practice to the child and parent. The analogy of learning a sport or a musical instrument can be helpful here. Most children are aware that they have improved in a sport/instrument since first trying it because they have practiced it. Similarly, we explain that as they practice this new relaxation skill they will likewise improve. Moreover, sports people don't just show up at their matches, they go to training, while musicians don't just show up to perform in recitals or concerts, they practice. In the same way, we need to train and practice our relaxation skills when we are calm so that we are well-practiced before our "match" or "concert"—that is, when we are scared or angry.

Mindfulness training with children has been becoming increasingly popular. While there is a growing body of evidence supporting the efficacy of mindfulness-based interventions in improving emotion regulation in adults, research with children is only in its early stages (Burke 2010; Zelazo and Lyons 2011). Clinically, we have found mindfulness practice to be a helpful component of our therapy with some of the children and families we see. Some children are already familiar with mindfulness from its application at their school, which assists in normalizing its use and provides opportunities for ongoing practice. We find that children often engage better in brief mindfulness practices than in longer sitting practices. For example, just closing their eyes, placing their hands on their tummy (or perhaps one on their tummy and one on their chest) and noticing several breaths along with the movement of their tummy as they breathe is a nice brief practice.

There are now many commercially available resources with a variety of mindfulness practices developed for children. For example, in *Sitting Still Like a Frog: Mindfulness Exercises for Kids (and Their Parents)*, Snel (2013) introduces parents to using mindfulness at home, and provides recordings of simple meditations of varying lengths for children to practice. We find it helpful to encourage parents to also engage in these brief mindfulness practices with their children, as they may likewise benefit. If you, or the parents or teachers you work with, are interested in introducing mindfulness to children, other helpful resources can be found in Etty-Leal (2010) and Kaiser Greenland (2010). There are also some useful mindfulness apps suitable for children.

One aspect of mindfulness work that is often helpful is when children gain an understanding of the transient nature of feelings and thoughts. When a child is distressed, they often feel as though that emotion will last forever. Similarly, when a child is thinking a distressing thought, they may consider it a fact that they will always think and believe. It is helpful for children to understand that feelings and thoughts come and go from our minds, that they will pass. It is also helpful for children to understand that even difficult emotions may be a normal response that we cannot just *stop* ourselves from experiencing. In fact, sometimes the efforts of children and parents to avoid or stop feelings serves to create further anxiety. Our activities *Feeling bubbles* and *Disappearing thoughts and feelings* were both developed as hands-on ways of exploring these concepts with children. Understanding that feelings come and go is a core component of ACT. For example, Hayes and Ciarrochi's (2015) ACT model incorporates "noticing" skills, such as observing and allowing inner experiences to come and go, rather than trying to change or cling to these experiences.

Another lovely activity for exploring these concepts, and for introducing mindfulness to children, is the "Mind Jar" or "Mind in a Jar" which has been described by Hanh (2011) and MacLean (2009) and adapted by others. This activity uses water in a vase, jar or bottle to represent the mind and added glitter or sand to represent different types of thoughts or feelings, which are all shaken up when we are upset or have a busy mind. It provides an opportunity to reflect on how the feelings settle down when our mind is clear and calm. This is an engaging visual analogy to assist in talking about the ideas that all feelings are okay and normal, that they do come and go again, and that it is difficult to think clearly when they are all shaken up. We like to reflect on how we can't just force the glitter to settle down, but how we can look after ourselves while it's all shaken up. If you are interested in using a similar activity, Kerry Lee MacLean's (2009) delightful story about a moody cow who learns to meditate incorporates her mind jar activity. Alternatively, an online search for feelings glitter bottles will reveal some different methods.

Other behavioral coping strategies

Many children respond well to more active behavioral strategies to manage big feelings such as anger and anxiety. Some commonly recommended strategies include engaging in a physical activity such as jumping on a trampoline, throwing a ball against a wall or star jumps, or simply walking away to engage in play elsewhere. Sensory activities such as fiddling with tactile toys or listening to music can also be calming for many children. Another helpful strategy involves the child communicating their feelings to a supportive person, such as a parent or teacher, either by talking or using a visual tool (e.g. a feelings chart or card), or simply seeking a hug.

Stress balls are a well-known, portable behavioral strategy. Children often enjoy making their own stress balls in therapy, which provides an engaging activity to complete while talking about stress, and a tactile reminder of the session to take home. Stress balls can be made by filling a balloon with rice, sand or flour using a funnel, and knotting the top. Some children like to decorate the ball using markers; for example, they may draw feelings faces or write helpful messages to remember when they are stressed. Others like to create interesting patterns by cutting the neck off another balloon as well as making some holes in it, and stretching it over the top of the stress ball. If you are interested in other variations and ideas for making stress balls you will find many online.

Simple behavioral strategies tend to be relatively easy for children to understand and parents often find them practical, both of which can help with engagement early in the therapy process (as compared to cognitive strategies). Some families, however, still require a considerable amount of work in order to implement behavioral strategies. Further, different families are likely to find different strategies helpful.

Role play and problem solving

Trying out new behavioral responses is an important process for children and parents in therapy. Within a CBT framework, this can be important in challenging and shifting unhelpful cognitions, and is also required for building skills in managing emotions, resolving conflicts or solving problems. Trying new behaviors and finding new ways to be in the world is also a core component in Hayes and Ciarrochi's (2015) ACT model for youth—that is, their "discoverer" space.

Role play provides an excellent way to model other strategies for children and to have them try out alternative behaviors. Playing with dolls, figures, puppets or toy animals is a great way to engage children in role play, providing them with the opportunity to practice within a safe environment. Altering the scenario so that it resembles what the child is struggling with often helps children to feel more comfortable about engaging in the play. For example, constructing a scenario about a new animal arriving at the zoo can be helpful for a child who has just started at a new school and has anxiety around how to initiate play with other children. *Which animal?* is an activity that draws on play to help children think about and try out different behavioral responses to challenging situations. *Rocket chair* is another activity that allows children to use their discoverer space and explore different ways of responding. Older children may enjoy creating videos of role plays on a tablet.

Role play provides a way of reality testing within the safety of the therapy session and can be used to gently challenge a child's unhelpful thoughts through experiences in play rather than through conversation. Reality testing, or exposure tasks, are often something we agree children will try at home between sessions and role play provides an opportunity for rehearsal prior to engaging in exposure tasks at home. Several of our activities encourage children, together with their families, to experiment and reality test through play in order to address specific anxieties, either in session (*Scary sounds game*) or at home (*Mad Monday; Mistake jars; Monster hunt*).

Teaching problem solving is also a common focus of therapy, with the model varying to fit with the child's developmental level. For example, Peterson and Adderley have developed a stop, think, do approach to problem solving that is often utilized with children in a school context (see Peterson and Adderley 2002) and problem-solving skills training is often included in CBT programs (Barrett 1999; Stallard 2002). Role play provides an opportunity to stop and think as the play progresses about the choices the child might make. You can further extend on problem solving by having a child rate how helpful the response was—for example, they could give each option a thumbs up or down or score it out of ten. *Possibilities jump* introduces problem solving to children in a concrete, hands-on manner, and also encourages children to try out new behavioral responses.

Helpful and unhelpful thoughts

Helping children to identify their thoughts is an important part of therapy. Young children often find identifying thoughts difficult; however, touching on this in therapy is helpful, as discussed in Chapter 5. For older children, being able to identify their own thoughts as well as those of others is often very helpful in assisting them to understand situations and think about alternative ways of responding. Drawing thought bubbles to make thoughts overt can be helpful, as can articulating our own thoughts during therapy.

A central component of cognitive therapies is helping children to understand that thoughts influence feelings, and that thoughts may or may not be true or helpful. At a very simple level, many young children can learn helpful things to say to themselves, or positive self-talk. For children who are able to articulate their unhelpful thoughts learning to manage these thoughts can be an important part of therapy. Sometimes managing this means noticing the unhelpful thoughts as they occur, accepting them as simply thoughts (not facts), and understanding that they will pass, consistent with an ACT framework. Sometimes it is about being able to argue against these thoughts or gather evidence to challenge these thoughts, as in a traditional CBT approach.

A simple approach to exploring thoughts and encouraging cognitive change with older children makes use of thought bubbles and the idea of unhelpful and helpful thoughts. We ask the child to draw their face expressing the emotion they are struggling with (i.e. looking angry, sad or scared) on one piece of paper, and consider the thoughts that often make them feel that way, writing each one in a thought bubble around the face. We generally label these thoughts as unhelpful thoughts, because they make us feel worse, but we emphasize that they are not bad thoughts and that we all experience thoughts like these sometimes. We would then ask the child to draw their face looking neutral or a little happy, and write in some helpful thoughts—that is, thoughts that help them feel better. Sometimes asking the child what they would tell a friend in that situation can help them to generate helpful thoughts. Both types of thoughts can be further explored in terms of the effects they have on the child's feelings and behavior, how true or realistic the thoughts are, how much the child believes the thoughts, and so on.

Although we tend to prefer the labels "helpful" and "unhelpful" thoughts, we would modify this language to fit best with the child and family's own language and understanding whenever appropriate. Some families may prefer to talk about negative and positive thoughts, or realistic thoughts. Others may prefer to call them calm thoughts and angry/worry thoughts, or about hot thoughts and cool thoughts (used by Stallard 2002). We would avoid calling them good and bad thoughts though, to avoid the implication that unhelpful thoughts are "bad" in the sense of naughty or harmful.

In Chapter 5, when considering the implications of developmental level for therapy, we talked about the use of cognitive strategies with younger and older children. A number of our activities also focus on these strategies. *Treasure chest*, *Magic spell*, *Thoughts to stick with* and *Helpful thought bracelet* were all developed to explain and encourage the use of helpful thoughts. *Disappearing thoughts and feelings* and *Strain it out* encourage letting go of unhelpful thoughts, while *Kick-back soccer* and *Colored glasses* focus on managing unhelpful thoughts by countering them with more realistic or helpful thoughts.

Narrative ideas and externalizing the problem

As discussed previously, we often involve children in externalizing conversations and find this very helpful clinically. Externalizing involves naming the problem and, in doing so, separates the problem from the child, empowering them and their family to approach it in a different manner. For example, a child might refer to their anger as the explosion monster or their anxiety as the wobbles. Listening carefully to the language that the child and family use and engaging them in an externalizing conversation is often one of the first therapeutic interventions that we use, typically occurring during the assessment. Further information about how to use externalizing conversations can be found in White and Morgan (2006). Programs such as "Talking Back to OCD" (March and Benton 2006) utilize this approach and it is often particularly helpful for developing the motivation of a child and family to work on a problem. The activities *What lives in your house?* and *Worry box* both involve some externalizing conversation.

Sometimes we use drawing to help children externalize their problem. This may be as simple as asking the child to draw a picture of the problem. Geldard *et al.* (2013) describe the "monster-in-me" strategy which involves externalizing a child's behavioral problem by discussing with them the monster that lives inside of them that gets them in trouble. They ask the child to draw the monster, and then build further on this in therapy to help the child recognize that they can be the boss of the monster and control their behavior. We use a similar activity in addressing anxiety, in which we ask the child to draw what their worry would look like if it was a monster. Helping them to draw the monster often engages them in some discussion about what the monster does and how it makes them feel. For example, a child might say that their worry monster has a big stick and pokes them in the stomach or that it says terrible things to them. The focus of our conversation turns to how the child can fight off the monster, putting them in a position of control rather than frightening them.

Using strengths and promoting resilience

A number of therapeutic approaches incorporate interventions aimed at identifying and using a child and family's strengths. Hayes and Ciarrochi's (2015) ACT model incorporates guiding young people to discover and test their strengths. Narrative approaches also often focus on highlighting an individual's strengths and creating a more positive story. Drawing out the strengths of a child and family is something we try to do during the assessment phase, highlighting these in our feedback to the family. In doing so, we may reflect on how they can use these skills in overcoming their difficulties and we can promote optimism and resilience. Asking the family to take it in turns to say one thing they are doing well and one thing they enjoy that they would like to do more of is a helpful way of reflecting on strengths and values, as is the activity *In my heart*. Strength cards can provide a helpful visual tool for reflecting on strengths of a child or family.

One activity that we like to use to explore and reinforce strengths is asking the child to consider what sort of superhero they would be if they were a superhero. It is similar to an activity called "If I were a superhero" outlined by Kelsey (2008) in which the child is asked to pretend they are a superhero that has never been invented before with the aim of assessing their coping mechanisms. The child considers what they would look like, what their superpowers would be and how they would use them, then draws their superhero in action. We extend on this by asking the child to consider which would be their strongest power and which would be the most helpful in managing their difficulties. We also ask them about any super-friends who would help them (who they would be and how they would help) as well as any enemies and how the enemies would try to attack them. In doing so, we can assist the child to develop a positive narrative that is symbolic of themself and their ability to cope with their current difficulties. Superhero themes can also be readily extended into comic strips that we make with the child, choosing a theme that reflects something they find difficult and developing an alternate story. For example, we've written comic adventures about themes such as "Starman and the Colossal Assignment" for a child struggling with school stress, and "Purple Girl Undercover at the Big Party" for a child with social anxiety.

Throughout therapy, reflecting regularly on progress and even small successes helps to build a child's understanding of their strengths and motivation for further change. The activities *Breaking news...* and *What lives in your house?* can provide engaging ways to review a child's and family's progress. It is also helpful to reflect on strengths at the end of therapy, to reinforce new skills and strategies they have developed and to promote resilience.

Consolidating coping strategies

It is often helpful for children to have their coping strategies made explicit and presented in a visual or hands-on format. This may be a "calm box" filled with calming, hands-on materials for younger children. Older children may prefer a variation such as a collection of cards on a keyring or lanyard, with images or words to represent their coping strategies. A number of CBT programs with children utilize a similar intervention. For example, Attwood (2004) introduces the notion of an emotional toolkit, which is a list of physical activities, relaxing activities, social tools, thinking tools and other tools that a child can use when they are worried or angry. Thomas (2009) uses a similar idea which she calls a Coping Skills Tool Box.

We find developing a calm box to be a very useful intervention with children to assist with generalization of coping strategies to other environments and to reinforce the strategies they have learnt. It is also an activity that can be easily varied for children of differing developmental levels and interests. For these reasons, although similar interventions are presented elsewhere, we have described our *Calm box* activity in Part II to share how we introduce and use this activity and to present creative ideas for variations. Other activities that can be used to bring together coping strategies include *Board games* and *Bowl it over*.

Home activities (not homework)

Practice is an important component of CBT and we use home activities routinely with the children and families we work with. Home activities can help generalize learning from therapy into the home environment and provide children with an opportunity to use strategies in context. Because the therapy environment is a safe one, in which children generally don't become too scared or angry, home practice is essential. It provides children with an awareness of their feelings and thoughts as they occur and allows them to try out strategies they have learnt in the clinic room.

Home activities also provide more opportunities for practice, which is important when learning new skills. Further, they can increase the involvement of family members who have not been involved in sessions. Indeed the process of sending a child home with an activity is also symbolic of what we want to happen in therapy—we want to teach the child and the family some new skills that they can use and integrate into their daily life.

Explaining that you will use home activities and sharing your rationale for this is important early in therapy. It is part of setting up the expectation that parents will be actively involved in the therapy and will remain focused on their goals between sessions. We often talk with parents about how much more time children spend at home and how different home is to the clinic room. We talk about the need to practice the skills they learn in context and to involve other family members. If a family feels daunted by this then we explain that we will negotiate home activities with them and that we will try to choose activities that readily fit into their daily routine or require only a brief amount of time.

In our experience most parents are very happy to be actively involved in their child's therapy and are very open to completing home activities.

We tend to use the term home activity rather than homework because of the negative connotations homework has for many children. While we view home activities as very important, we tend to keep these simple. Often taking home something they have done in a session is enough. If children are taking something home we encourage them to show it to another family member, rather than simply leave it in the car or drop it on the table when they walk in the door. The physical process of taking something home is symbolic of the learning being transferred from the clinic room to home and for this reason we try to have children take home items that are meaningful or that they will be keen to show to another family member. Often this means that the child does not take home everything they have done in the session. Rather we choose something that exemplifies the core concept or skill we have worked on. We support the child to take home what they have created by talking with them about where they will put it and what they will do with it. For example, we might ask who they will show it to and what they think the response will be.

Some therapists use therapy boxes or books containing all the work a child completes in therapy. Indeed, we have used this idea from time to time too. Generally, though, we find that the message we want to give children and their parents is that therapy is something to be taken home rather than something that remains in the clinic room until therapy is completed. Sending the child home from a session with a picture or model they have created reinforces the link between therapy sessions and the home environment.

Sometimes if you feel a child is really struggling to generalize what they learn in sessions to home, you might like to pop their drawings in the mail to them. Children adore getting mail and all you need to do is jot a quick note saying you are looking forward to seeing them again and put some stickers on the envelope and you have something they can't ignore. Parents often describe how happy their child was to receive the letter and how they sat and looked at it together. The technique of therapeutic letter writing was developed by White and Epston (1990) and interested readers may like to read the recent chapter by Bjoroy, Madigan and Nylund (2015), which provides an excellent summary of this technique along with some helpful examples. We see this as a valuable strategy, and there is a body of literature supporting it (see Fox 2003 for a review). Therapeutic letter writing is, however, time-consuming and while it is something we use in our practice we do so less frequently. Posting a child's drawing is far less time-consuming, though it seems to be helpful.

As mothers we are very mindful of the time constraints faced by families and try to keep our home activities manageable for families. The sorts of activities we use tend to be playing a game we used in therapy, exploring a new app related to the therapy, reading a relevant book together, or practicing breathing or relaxation skills. Home activities can also be used to shift the focus away from the problem. You can, for example, ask parents to note down times when the child is brave or to have a special play time with the child prior to the next session. We might also suggest that the family hang something we made in our session on the fridge or note something on the family calendar to serve as a reminder about the home activity. We ensure that the family have any materials they need or can readily obtain them.

Scheduling sessions sufficiently far apart can allow families to do what you have asked before the next session. Weekly sessions can be helpful for some families in the earliest stages while still building rapport. However, generally we find that fortnightly sessions work well. A week seems to come around so quickly that often families have not had time to reflect on what you spoke about and try something different.

It is important that you make some time in the next session to talk about the home activity that you asked the family to complete. You might choose to review this with the whole family or with the parents alone, depending on how you want to structure this session. We try to be positive about anything the family has attempted and if the family has not been able to attempt the task we spend some time talking about it, drawing on what they noticed so that there is some therapeutic benefit. Families are often experiencing a lot of failure by the time they come to therapy so we avoid any judgment when they are unable to complete home activities.

Helpful ideas for working with children
Using popular culture and a child's interests

We often find that having children of our own helps enormously in that we tend to know what the latest craze is. Not only does being able to ask a relevant question about the latest thing prove your credentials to the child, it also provides opportunities for using this toy, hobby, movie or book in therapy.

Learning about some of the child's interests during the assessment phase is important for assessment and engagement. Expressing a curiosity is often enough and you don't generally need to go out and research the latest toy or movie. If, however, you are finding the child is difficult to engage, you may want to do a bit of research so that you can find ideas for incorporating their interests into therapy.

Hearing about a child's favorite TV show or movie and finding out about their favorite character and what they like about that character is often helpful as it can lead to activities or metaphors that you can use in therapy. Asking the child to choose a character that is most like each member of their family can provide you with some valuable information.

Popular children's movies and books often have a helpful message that may be relevant for therapy. Consider Disney's *Finding Nemo* or *Inside Out*, movies that contain positive messages about feelings. These movies can prompt discussion, normalize experiences and be the basis for engaging activities around feelings. Many of the toys marketed for boys are polarized into good and evil and engage in battle. *Star Wars* is a great example of this. This concept lends itself well for talking about the battle between helpful and unhelpful thoughts.

Therapeutic books

Books are a wonderful resource when working with children. Listening to storybooks and discussing them is a familiar and enjoyable activity for many children of all ages. Books are often used in psychoeducation, to build emotional vocabulary and understanding of emotions. Books also normalize the experience of different emotions, and help children to realize they are not alone and to identify with others. Further, books can assist in opening up conversations about feelings and experiences in a non-confronting and comfortable way, helping children to think about and express their own feelings. For older children, books can provide a collaborative way to find new ideas that they think they might like to try.

There are a number of books that were written with a therapeutic goal of assisting children in managing emotions or specific difficulties. More generally, however, children's books that include a character who experiences an emotion that the child is finding difficult are helpful, as are those where the problem is similar to the one experienced by the child. Geldard *et al.* (2013) provide a detailed description of their use of storybooks in therapy.

We sometimes read short books together with children in therapy sessions, while prompting them to consider the feelings and thoughts of characters. This may lead to helping the child to make connections to their own experiences (for example, asking "Is that what it's like for you when you feel…" "Is that something you'd like to try?"). Longer books could be lent out or recommended for home, to encourage further conversation on the topic at home, or to allow the child and parent to review or extend session content. We have included a list of our favorite books for use in therapy with children as an appendix.

Making your own stories and books

Storytelling is a strong component of narrative therapy and it lends itself beautifully to working with children. Burns (2005) provides comprehensive information on using storytelling in therapy with children and detailed advice for creating therapeutic stories (as well as many ready-made stories too). Geldard *et al.* (2013) and Cattanach (2008) also describe a number of different strategies therapists can use for storytelling with children, which are very much worth reading if you are not familiar with this technique. Essentially, the important aspects of storytelling are that the therapist works with the child to construct a narrative that the child identifies with in some way. Typically the child will identify with one of the characters or with the problem outlined in the story. The story is therapeutic because it provides the child with other possibilities and an alternative ending. Stories can be enacted with puppets or toys, told, recorded or written down.

We particularly like writing and illustrating stories with children as we find they create a good resource for the child and family. They are easy to take home and read to others and can be re-read as desired or needed. We tend to write stories in collaboration with children, choosing a character who in some way relates to the child and a problem that is similar to what the child is facing. For example, with Mackenzie who was anxious about doing the wrong thing in class and was asking excessive questions of her teacher, we wrote a story called "Mack's Facts." The story summarized what she had learnt about how asking questions increased, rather than decreased, her anxiety and listed some of the strategies she had practiced in sessions.

Some children will be very happy to create a handwritten book while others will prefer to use the computer or a tablet. There are a number of book-making apps that can make this lots of fun, allowing you to upload photos or videos and record the child's voice as they tell the story.

Using and making games

Games can be a nice way of building rapport with children. Geldard *et al.* (2013) describe in detail their use of games when counseling children. We tend to choose games like Jenga, Noughts and Crosses or Connect Four, as children are generally able to talk while playing these and they are quick to play. Alternatively, there are a number of therapeutic games on the market that can be purchased for use with children. Sometimes having a ready-made game reassures children that there are others with similar difficulties and often they can be a good icebreaker for children who are reluctant to answer questions or participate in play activities. As a therapist, these games are generally easy to use and require little preparation.

A number of therapists have outlined strategies for making games in therapy. For example, see the Snakes and Ladders game described by Hobday and Ollier (2005). Making your own games together in therapy is often very useful and children generally find it fun. This allows for the game to be individualized according to the child's interests and therapeutic needs and taken home to aid generalization. The process of creating the game also provides a non-confronting context for therapeutic conversations about emotions and strategies. The activity *Board games* describes how we go about making games with children to assess or review their strategies for managing emotions or to explore helpful versus unhelpful responses.

CHAPTER 7

How to Use the Activities in This Book

Part II of this book contains a number of activities that can be used therapeutically with children. These activities are not, however, presented in the form of a standardized program. This chapter describes how you can use your understanding of a child to choose appropriate activities, how to modify and implement activities, and how to begin developing your own activities.

Choosing activities

Each of the activities in this book begins with a brief introduction incorporating the aim of the activity. This allows you to determine whether the aim fits with your formulation and treatment plan and to assist you in choosing an appropriate activity. Some of the activities will be appropriate for many of the children you see. For example, many children benefit from expressing feelings (such as in *Feeling block people*), from recognizing progress (as in *Breaking news…*) and from articulating helpful thoughts (as in *Treasure chest*). Other activities, however, such as the *Mistake jars* or *Scary sounds game*, have a more specific focus and will only be appropriate for children who experience those specific difficulties. It is essential that you use your assessment of your client and your clinical judgment to decide whether an activity is likely to be therapeutic with your client at that time.

We realized that categorizing the activities, such as by age or by intervention, would help readers quickly find appropriate activities when planning sessions. However, categorizing the activities as such can be somewhat limiting. Many activities can be used for several therapeutic interventions and modified for different developmental levels and presenting problems. For example, although we would categorize *Target practice* as a scaling activity, it also incorporates recognizing and expressing feelings, and building coping strategies, and can be used with younger and older children to help with anger or anxiety.

To help you find activities to consider for particular interventions, we have put together a quick reference guide at the end of this chapter in Table 7.1. This table links each of the activities with the key components of therapy discussed previously. Using this table as a guide you will be able to select appropriate activities, using these flexibly and adapting them to address various therapeutic goals and meet the needs of your individual clients. We have provided examples below of how three of the activities could be modified for differing presenting problems, developmental levels and individual needs. We would suggest that you read through the activities in Part II and then have a look over these examples in order to help you think about how to adapt the activities for the children you are working with.

MAGIC SPELL

Susie was a five-year-old girl with an ASD who benefitted from the *Magic spell* activity. In addition to her ASD, Susie experienced social anxiety and was very fearful of meeting new people, which often resulted in angry outbursts and running away. She enjoyed making a wand, with her magic spell simply being "I will be okay." When Susie joined a new dance class, her mother was able to talk with her about how she might feel shy and what she could do. They practiced saying her magic spell in the lead up to going to the group and Susie was able to attend the class without any of the difficulties that were typically associated with her meeting new people.

In working with Susie, the therapist was mindful that her ASD and her young age limited her ability to engage in flexible thinking. For this reason the helpful thought (or magic spell) was kept simple and was practiced with her mother. The act of physically waving the wand and practicing the spell was developmentally appropriate, fitting with a young child's need for activity, and also served as a useful distraction from Susie's anxiety.

Lucy was an eight-year-old typically developing girl, who experienced significant generalized anxiety, along with some social anxiety. Her parents often responded by providing a lot of reassurance and were generally able to talk her through difficult situations. She struggled at school, however, often becoming tearful and frequently seeking out teachers. Lucy enjoyed craft and loved making things in therapy. The *Magic spell* activity was used to help her reflect on the words that we say to ourselves and how helpful they can be. Lucy was able to generate magic spells that would be ideal for a variety of situations that the therapist introduced using puppets. For example, she was able to say a magic spell for situations in which a puppet might worry about not having anyone to play with ("I usually can find someone to play with") or completing schoolwork ("Everyone makes mistakes"). This activity was used in combination with other activities aimed at developing helpful thoughts and, as therapy progressed, Lucy displayed a much more positive thinking pattern.

In working with Lucy, the therapist was able to utilize Lucy's ability to generate helpful thoughts in a flexible manner to help her think about how she could apply these to situations that she often experienced. Using puppet play enabled Lucy to have some hands-on practice, increasing the likelihood that she would be able to apply her knowledge outside of the clinic room.

BOWL IT OVER

Matthew was a four-year-old typically developing boy, who experienced separation anxiety upon commencing preschool. He had a very close relationship with his mother, who described herself as having mild anxiety, and it was his first experience of separating from her. *Bowl it over* was used once he and his mother had been engaged in therapy for some time and he had been able to separate without too much distress. Matthew and his mother generated a number of problems, which the therapist wrote down for the bowling pins. These included "Matthew crying and holding onto Mum," "Mum worrying whether Matthew will be okay" and "Matthew being too worried to play at kinder." Together with the therapist they came up with ideas about how they had been able to get past these problems. These included Mum spending some time playing with Matthew at preschool, having a special way of saying goodbye and helping Matthew remember that Mum would be coming back. The therapist was able to reflect on how brave Matthew had been and help him to rate how worried he used to feel as opposed to how worried he now felt. Matthew enjoyed bowling the pins over and his mother was able to reflect on what she had done which had been helpful. The therapist was able to help them reflect on how similar strategies might work should Matthew experience anxiety in the future.

In the above example, the therapist was able to work therapeutically with both Matthew and his mother. Praising Matthew and reflecting on his success was important and helped him begin to create a narrative about himself as someone who was brave, as opposed to worried. Empowering his mother by reflecting on what she had been able to achieve reinforced her role as an effective and capable parent and prepared her to terminate therapy.

Jane was a ten-year-old girl with a mild ID, a significant language disorder and associated learning difficulties. She found school extremely challenging and often avoided completing work. Homework was also quite frustrating and anxiety-provoking for her and often resulted in Jane becoming angry, which led to lots of conflict within the family. She had attended five sessions of therapy and had worked with the therapist on a number of strategies that she could use to manage her anxiety and anger. *Bowl it over* was used to help Jane recall and consolidate these strategies. Jane and the therapist used some clear plastic cups to make pins, and inserted into each a piece of card that had a difficulty she experienced written on it. These included writing, homework and swimming. The therapist wrote these down for Jane, knowing that asking her to write often raised her anxiety and led to frustration. The therapist had Jane say something that helped her to deal with these difficulties prior to rolling the ball and trying to hit some of the pins over. Therapy had centered on behavioral strategies, such as asking for help, having a go and taking a deep breath, along with some simple helpful thoughts, such as "I can try." Jane reflected on these when bowling over the pins. On one occasion she did not hit any pins and this provided a good opportunity to talk about how sometimes you can try something and it doesn't work. The therapist was able to suggest that she could try again or try something different, describing how in this way the game could be similar to real life.

In working with Jane, the therapist was mindful of the need to use simple language and to emphasize behavioral strategies. Where a helpful thought was introduced, it was kept simple and chosen to be applicable across all of the difficult situations Jane identified. The activity provided a helpful way for Jane to practice her strategies, with the therapist recognizing that she was likely to need more practice than a typically developing child.

THOUGHTS TO STICK WITH

Sam was an eight-year-old boy with a language disorder and associated difficulties with literacy. He experienced generalized anxiety, worrying about things such as the school concert and the flying fox at camp even when these situations were months away. Therapy had focused on helping Sam better understand and articulate his feelings. The therapist had focused on behavioral strategies with an emphasis on helping Sam face his fears in small steps while assisting him to manage his anxiety. Sam had struggled to engage in cognitive strategies, appearing to find the language and flexible thinking required too challenging. Following some progress in therapy, the therapist was able to help Sam make a magnet with a thought that he found helpful and would like to stick with. Sam was able to suggest "Try it and you won't be worried anymore," which the therapist transcribed onto a magnet and which Sam proudly displayed on his fridge. He was able to remind his mother of this on a few occasions, directing her attention to the magnet when she appeared worried.

In working with Sam, the therapist focused on behavioral strategies, recognizing that his language skills limited his ability to engage in cognitive therapy. The therapist later capitalized on what he had learnt through trying those things he was worried about, creating a visual reminder that both Sam and his parents could use when he experienced new situations.

Sarah was a 12-year-old girl with high-functioning ASD. She was experiencing anxiety and depression in the context of her upcoming transition to secondary school. Sarah loved anime and enjoyed drawing her favorite characters. She was able to reflect on helpful and unhelpful thoughts with the therapist and the therapist suggested that they make some magnets together, knowing that Sarah was likely to benefit from having some visual prompts of helpful thoughts. The therapist asked that Sarah draw some of her favorite characters on magnetic paper, giving each a speech bubble. Sarah and the therapist then worked together to generate some ideas about what these characters could say that might be helpful. One of the helpful thoughts Sarah generated was "You can't stop change. You just have to go with it." Sarah stuck these magnets on a whiteboard in her room and looked at them sometimes when she felt sad.

In working with Sarah, the therapist used her areas of interest to engage her, and in doing so, ensured that she would be motivated to complete the task. Sticking the magnets up in her bedroom enabled these to be a visual prompt, which many children with ASD find helpful.

How to use the activities

Each of the activities provides suggestions about what you might say to your client as you introduce and complete that activity. The activities also provide ideas about how to engage parents and many include developmental considerations and variations.

Our intention, however, is that you adapt these activities so that they are appropriate for the particular child and family that you are working with, your therapeutic objectives overall and that they are appropriate at that point in therapy, to your own skills and competencies, and to your workplace. This might involve substantial modifications to the activities or simply altering the language you use so that it matches that of your client. Modifying activities to incorporate a child's interests is also valuable, particularly if they are a reluctant participant in therapy.

The activities are designed to provide a way of introducing and explaining therapeutic concepts to children. It is, however, the pairing of these activities with therapeutic conversations and home activities that leads to change. For example, Isla, an eight-year-old with separation anxiety that manifested predominantly when she was put to bed at night and when her parents went into the backyard, benefitted from the *Magic cord* activity. While Isla clearly enjoyed the activity in the room, which involved asking her mother to go out into the hall to see if she could feel the pull on the cord, it was the conversation around this that was most helpful. In addition to the conversations the therapist had with Isla during the session, her parents both continued the conversation with her at home and encouraged her to remember the magic cord when needed. Isla also returned happily to each of the following sessions to tell the therapist about all the times she had been able to remember about the magic cord.

Activities that focus on feelings within families

All of the activities in this book are able to be completed with active involvement of parents and other family members. If you choose to do the activity with the child individually, our recommendation is that you discuss and share this with the family and we have outlined some suggestions for doing so. There are, however, some additional activities that we have included that focus specifically on feelings within families. The emphasis in these activities is on recognizing how other family members are feeling and understanding some of the dynamics that occur within the family when emotions are heightened. These activities explore concepts such as the notion that feelings can be contagious and the idea that one person's feelings affect others. They include *Feelings in our family*, *What lives in your house?*, *Family feelings jump*, *Yawn game* and *Family feelings inventory*.

It is important to understand that these are not the only activities we would have you use when the whole family is present. We have used many of the other activities during family sessions and have designed all so that they can be used in this way.

Knowing when to use activities with families

The activities included in the book are for families who you are actively involved in therapy with. These are families with whom you have completed a thorough assessment and developed therapeutic goals. There will no doubt be times when you have families who are ambivalent about coming to therapy and are still in the early stages of engagement. Rushing these families into active therapy is often problematic and can, for example, lead to some of what you work on in sessions being undermined. If you are concerned about a family's level of engagement, we would encourage you to focus on this first, perhaps using a motivational interviewing approach or similar.

New therapists can find it frustrating when their caseload consists of a number of families who are not yet therapy-ready. Often they are eager to try all of the creative ideas they have learnt about and may engage children and parents in therapy sessions too early, which can be problematic.

Appropriately timing therapeutic interventions and activities involves informed clinical decisions. We encourage you to consider your formulation of each client in making these decisions. Sometimes you will need to focus on other factors first, either within your therapy sessions (for example, difficulties in parenting or the parent-child relationship) or by referral elsewhere (for example, to address parental mental health concerns or marital difficulties).

Creating activities

Most of our ideas for activities come from the children we work with. Often it is the way they express something in a session or a metaphor that comes to mind as we begin to understand their difficulties that forms the basis of our ideas. We link this with our understanding of what is going on for the child (our formulation) and our aim for what we want the activity to achieve (our therapy goals).

Sometimes our ideas come from playing with our own children or our observations of them. For example, watching our children make a volcano using a science kit enabled us to think about how we might use this therapeutically. In situations like this it is the way we use the activity and how we talk about it that has therapeutic value rather than the activity itself.

When we develop an activity during a session we find that it sometimes doesn't quite work and that we need to think further about how we explain or implement it. Usually, however, we are able to find another way of conveying the concept that we wanted to explain to the child and we can modify the activity and try it again the following session if need be. The child also has an opportunity to see that we can make mistakes too, which is valuable learning.

Developing activities in this manner becomes easier with experience and therapists do naturally vary in their ability to develop new creative ideas. Many of the therapists who attend our workshops feel less confident in developing their own activities and are therefore eager to learn about commercially available books or activities that can assist them in their work. Others find they draw inspiration from the aisle of their local art and craft shop, using the resources there as a starting point for developing activities. It is helpful to know about your own individual preferences and consider what helps you most in your work.

Over to you

It is hoped that reading through this first part of the book has provided you with a good grounding in working with children if you are new to child work. If you are an experienced therapist, we hope that you have been able to reflect on why you practice the way you do.

Perhaps you have even thought of something you would like to do differently in future. We hope that the activities that follow in the next section help you to add to your therapy toolbox and that they are well suited to the children that you see. Perhaps these activities will inspire you to create some new activities of your own or to share the activities you already use with others.

Table 7.1 Quick reference guide to activities

Therapeutic approach	Activities	Emotional difficulties
Recognizing and expressing feelings	Binoculars for looking inside (page 94)	Anxiety/anger/sadness
	Feeling block people (page 127)	Anxiety/anger/sadness
	Feelings buzzer (page 132)	Anxiety/anger/sadness
	Pushing my buttons (page 161)	Anxiety/anger/sadness
	Body mapping (page 101)	Anger/anxiety
	Target practice (page 172)	Anger/anxiety
	Warning signs (page 180)	Anger/anxiety
	Big volcano (page 92)	Anger
	Put the fire out (page 164)	Anger
	Straw that broke the camel's back (page 171)	Anger
	Butterfly catching (page 109)	Anxiety (worries)
	Worry box (page 186)	Anxiety (worries)
	Family feelings inventory (page 120)	Anxiety/anger/sadness (feelings within family)
	Family feelings jump (page 122)	Anxiety/anger/sadness (feelings within family)
Recognizing and expressing feelings; mixed and secondary emotions	Feelings juggle (page 136)	Anxiety/anger/sadness
	Feelings that show (page 138)	Anger
	Lift the flap on anger (page 148)	Anger
	Anxious/excited coin toss (page 90)	Anxiety (new events or challenges)
	Feelings in our family (page 134)	Anxiety/anger/sadness (feelings within family)
	Yawn game (page 188)	Anxiety/anger/sadness (feelings within family)

Therapeutic approach	Activities	Emotional difficulties
Recognizing bodily sensations (and thoughts)	Binoculars for looking inside (page 94)	Anxiety/anger/sadness
	Feelings buzzer (page 132)	Anxiety/anger/sadness
	Body mapping (page 101)	Anger/anxiety
	Put the fire out (page 164)	Anger
Scaling	Feelings thermometer (page 140)	Anger/anxiety
	Target practice (page 172)	Anger/anxiety
	Warning signs (page 180)	Anger/anxiety
	Big volcano (page 92)	Anger
	Put the fire out (page 164)	Anger
	Straw that broke the camel's back (page 171)	Anger
	Toilet paper scaling (page 176)	Anger
	Fear hierarchy (page 124)	Anxiety
Relaxation, breathing and mindfulness	Calm box (page 112)	Anger/anxiety/sadness
	Disappearing thoughts and feelings (page 118)	Anxiety/anger/sadness
	Feeling bubbles (page 130)	Anxiety/anger/sadness
	Blow your worries away (page 96)	Anger/anxiety
Role play and problem solving	Possibilities jump (page 160)	Anxiety/anger/sadness
	Rocket chair (page 166)	Anxiety/anger/sadness
	Which animal? (page 184)	Anxiety/anger/sadness
	Mad Monday (page 150)	Anxiety (things being imperfect or not right)
	Mistake jars (page 156)	Anxiety (making mistakes)
	Monster hunt (page 158)	Anxiety (fear of monsters)
	Scary sounds game (page 167)	Anxiety (fear of night noises)
Helpful and unhelpful thoughts	Helpful thought bracelet (page 143)	Anxiety/anger/sadness
	Magic spell (page 154)	Anxiety/anger/sadness
	Thoughts to stick with (page 174)	Anxiety/anger/sadness
	Treasure chest (page 178)	Anxiety/anger/sadness
	Colored glasses (page 115)	Anxiety/anger/sadness
	Disappearing thoughts and feelings (page 118)	Anxiety/anger/sadness
	Kick-back soccer (page 147)	Anxiety/anger/sadness
	Strain it out (page 169)	Anxiety/anger/sadness
	Monster hunt (page 158)	Anxiety (fear of monsters)
	Scary sounds game (page 167)	Anxiety (fear of night noises)

Narrative ideas and externalizing the problem	Bowl it over (page 105)	Anxiety/anger/sadness
	Big volcano (page 92)	Anger
	Put the fire out (page 164)	Anger
	Straw that broke the camel's back (page 171)	Anger
	Blow your worries away (page 96)	Anxiety
	Butterfly catching (page 109)	Anxiety (worries)
	Worry box (page 186)	Anxiety (worries)
	Magic cord (page 152)	Anxiety (separation anxiety)
	What lives in your house? (page 182)	Anxiety/anger/sadness (feelings within family)
Using strengths and promoting resilience	In my heart (page 145)	Anxiety/anger/sadness
	Breaking news... (page 107)	Anxiety/anger/sadness
	What lives in your house? (page 182)	Anxiety/anger/sadness (feelings within family)
Consolidating coping strategies	Board games (page 98)	Anxiety/anger/sadness
	Bowl it over (page 105)	Anxiety/anger/sadness
	Calm box (page 112)	Anxiety/anger/sadness

PART II

Creative Therapeutic Activities

In this second part of the book, we present in detail some of our favorite creative activities that we use in therapy sessions with children and families when treating emotional difficulties and building clients' skills in managing strong emotions.

Anxious/excited coin toss

Feeling anxious and excited often go together, particularly when children are faced with new events or challenges. Children who struggle with this anxiety often benefit from recognizing that it can be coupled with excitement, as well as exploring some of the functions of the anxiety and positives in these anxiety-provoking situations.

MATERIALS

» You will need a coin, some cardboard, glue, scissors and some markers.

PROCEDURE

Explain to the child that you have been thinking about some of their worries and wondering whether there are some other feelings that might go along with them. Say that you had to do something new on the weekend and felt both worried and excited about this. Suggest that you make a coin game to explore these feelings more.

Have the child draw a worried face and an excited face on the cardboard with marker pens. Cut the faces out with scissors and glue them on the opposite sides of a coin.

Use an example, such as needing to give a talk to a big group of people. Show the child the worried side of the coin while telling them a few worries you had (perhaps forgetting what you needed to say or mixing up your words). Then show the child the excited side and tell them what you were excited about (maybe sharing something that you found interesting).

Suggest that you play a game in which you think of a situation and flip the coin, taking it in turns to think about a worry or something exciting depending on how the coin lands.

Helpful examples include:

• going rock climbing

• talking at school assembly

• learning to rollerblade.

When the child understands the concept, ask if they can think of any times when they felt both excited and worried. Talk about whether there was more excitement or more worry. Ask about how excitement and worries feel in their body. Reflect on the way in which these feelings are similar or different for the child.

FOR PARENTS

Encourage the child to show the parent the coin game and see if their parent can think of an example of when they felt both worried and excited. Suggest the family take it home so family members can have a go at thinking of a time when they felt this way. See if you can reach a conclusion like "So it sounds like when most of us try something new we feel both excited and worried." Try to talk about the functional role of anxiety in new situations using terms the child can understand, such as "Maybe being a bit worried makes us really think about what we are doing so that we are safe and do our best."

DEVELOPMENTAL CONSIDERATIONS

Younger children can generally list situations that cause them to feel worried or excited. They are likely, however, to find it more difficult to think about both of these feelings in relation to the same situation. For this reason, it is useful to have a parent in the room when you do the activity to help the child think of situations when the child felt both anxious and excited and what these feelings related to. Older children will often be able to think about these examples without the support of a parent.

EXTENSION

This activity can readily be extended to talking about feelings in your body, discussing the role of avoidance, etc.

Big volcano

Many therapists use the metaphor of a volcano when talking with children about their anger (e.g. Stallard 2002). This activity makes use of the well-known science experiment of creating a volcanic eruption to explore anger with children. It provides a particularly engaging, visual and practical way of talking about anger, including the child's triggers and experiences of anger. It also incorporates scaling, helping the child to think about the different levels of anger.

MATERIALS

» You will need some air drying clay or play-doh to make a volcano out of.

» You will also need some bicarbonate of soda, white vinegar and food coloring.

» Having a small plastic medicine cup to sit inside the mouth of the volcano is helpful; however, making an indent with your fingers will also work.

» Finally, you will need a clear bucket, tub or large clear bowl to place the volcano in.

PROCEDURE

Explain to the child that some of the children you know seem to have anger that is like a great big volcano. You can explain what a volcano is if the child doesn't know. Ask if their anger ever feels like that. Explain that you can build a volcano while you think about this.

Make the volcano out of clay or play-doh and position the medicine cup in the mouth. Put the volcano inside the bucket or the bowl and put some bicarbonate of soda in the cup. Add a few drops of food color, asking the child what color they think the lava should be.

Provide the child with some examples of things that can make children angry and have them show you with their hands how angry this would make them feel. If it is something that makes them a little angry then say "Okay then, just a drop of vinegar for that" and for things that make them really angry add more vinegar. Make sure that you keep hold of the vinegar and that the child doesn't have their face close to the volcano. The volcano will erupt and you can talk about what this is like. For example, you can say "Wow, that just all came spilling out. Does your anger ever come out like that? What do you do if that happens?"

Children really like this experiment and often want to repeat it so you may choose to go through the process again. You can reflect as you mop up the first volcano about what might have helped it not to erupt and ask the child about anything that helps them to stay calm.

Most children readily appreciate the difference between the fun they experience in this activity and having their own meltdowns; however, if you feel the need, you can talk about how this is just a play volcano but how real volcanos hurt people, much in the way anger can.

The volcano can be taken home by the child to remind them of the therapeutic conversations and prompt them to share their learnings with other family members, both of which assist with generalization.

FOR PARENTS

This technique, of having children think about and show you with their hands how big a problem is, is a helpful one to encourage parents to use at home. It gives children something tangible to do, which provides a distraction and can help children evaluate the situation more realistically.

DEVELOPMENTAL CONSIDERATIONS

Most younger children will be able to understand this metaphor provided you are able to give examples. Having parents in the room is helpful as they will be able to suggest triggers that they have observed, helping the child begin to link the concept of the volcano with their own experiences. This activity is also generally enjoyed by older children.

Binoculars for looking inside

This activity helps build a child's awareness and understanding of their emotions, including the associated physiological and cognitive changes, as well as noticing and naming the emotion, which is important early in the therapy process.

MATERIALS

» You will need some toilet paper rolls or cardboard craft tubes, glue to stick them together and markers to decorate them.

» If you have some wool or cord handy it can be fun to connect this to the binoculars so that they can be worn around the child's neck.

PROCEDURE

Begin by suggesting that you make some binoculars from the rolls or tubes and glue, decorated with markers. Talk while you are making them about how binoculars work. Talk about how it is great to notice what is going on around you by looking closely; however, it is also important to notice what is happening inside of you. Suggest that you make these binoculars ones that are good for looking inside and discovering how you are feeling and what is happening in your body and your head.

When the binoculars are done give the child an example. Use the binoculars on yourself, scanning from your feet up and reflecting on what you notice in your body and finding a name for how you are feeling. Comment too on what your thoughts are. You can then ask the child to do the same.

Once the child has the idea you can talk about other examples. For instance, you might tell the child about a time that week when you felt worried and used the binoculars to scan yourself, explaining as you do what you noticed about your body (e.g. shaky hands and pounding heart) and in your head (i.e. a worried thought or "What if…"). Ask the child to think of a recent time when they felt sad, angry or worried (depending on the presenting problem) and use the binoculars to reflect on what they noticed in their body and head.

FOR PARENTS

Children can be encouraged to show these binoculars to their parents and teach them how to use them. Parents may be encouraged to try out the binoculars, to explore what emotions, body sensations and thoughts they are experiencing at the current moment, or what they would notice when experiencing a clinically relevant emotion.

Parents may reinforce these ideas at home when they notice their child experiencing an emotion, by asking the child to use their binoculars to see what they can notice in their body, head and feelings.

DEVELOPMENTAL CONSIDERATIONS

Varying your language should enable you to use this with both younger and older children. Younger children will benefit from having their parents involved to help provide examples of behaviors they notice at home.

Blow your worries away

Breathing techniques are generally effective, brief and portable relaxation strategies, and are used by most therapists. Releasing a deep breath can serve to calm a child's body down and to act as a helpful transition point, allowing them to pause and think. To learn about breathing, children usually need to be able to see the results of their out breath visually, and many therapists use bubbles to provide this visual feedback. The outline below describes how we do this, utilizing both breathing and some visual imagery to aid relaxation.

MATERIALS

- » You will need a bottle of bubbles.

- » It is also helpful to have small bottles of bubbles for children to take home.

PROCEDURE

Explain to the child that when you are worried or angry you tend to breathe differently. Explain that it can be helpful to blow your worries away and to do that you need to take a long breath out. Show the child how you can do this with a bottle of bubbles, encouraging them to watch while you blow the bubbles, saying "Look, all of my worries are floating away."

Allow the child to have a turn and encourage them to blow out slowly through their mouth, shaping this over a number of turns.

You can then talk with the child about whether they are allowed to blow bubbles at school or whether they always have bubbles close by. You can talk about how to blow pretend bubbles, showing the child how they can take a deep breath without the bubbles.

FOR PARENTS

Talk with parents about when they might need to blow their worries away and see if you can encourage children to prompt their parents to do so. Similarly, parents can practice breathing with children at home and can gently prompt their child to do so if they see them getting upset or angry.

DEVELOPMENTAL CONSIDERATIONS

Both younger and older children can benefit from learning to use a single deep breath. Using bubbles allows the child to see the product of their breath, providing clear feedback and enabling them to develop their technique. As such, even young children are able to learn how to breathe in a relaxing manner.

EXTENSION

Some children find the visual imagery of their worries floating away to be effective so it can be helpful to focus on this; others like the idea of the worries bursting. Encouraging children to imagine this when you blow the pretend bubbles can be helpful.

Breathing can be a particularly helpful strategy for children and can be integrated with other strategies. For example, learning to take a breath and think about what to do can be very helpful.

Board games

Therapists often make board games to provide an engaging way for children to express their feelings or learn and practice new skills within play. Children generally enjoy making their own game and identify more with their game than a pre-made or commercial game. What follows is a description of how we make board games with children, to help them identify helpful and unhelpful ways of managing their feelings. This activity can be used at the beginning of therapy with the aim of assessing the child's existing strategies and helping them to see that there are some alternative responses they can try. Alternatively, it can be used as a tool to review and reinforce strategies later in therapy.

MATERIALS

>> You will need a piece of card for the board, in A4 size or larger. Using paper then laminating it after completing the game also works well.

>> You may like to photocopy the game template provided in the *Board game template* on page 100 or to print a plain grid. An online search for "print free blank board game" will yield a number of other options.

>> You will need some markers or pencils to decorate the board, and possibly extra cardboard to cut for cards (optional).

>> Finally, you will need a dice and counters to play. It's helpful to have spares so that children can take them home with the game.

PROCEDURE

Ask the child if they would like to make a board game together. Use a game template or help the child to draw the squares on the card.

Talk to the child about their reason for coming to see you, and how you thought that together you could make a game to help with this. Assist the child to come up with a name for the game, perhaps suggesting some alternatives. For example, a child who is experiencing difficulties in managing their anger might make a game called Temper Trail.

Explain that the aim of the game will be to get from the start to the finish. Some squares will show helpful things to do when they are feeling angry (or scared/upset) and will let the child move forward. Other squares will have unhelpful things to do when they are feeling angry, and will move the child backwards.

Help the child to consider options for what they could do when feeling angry, and ask them whether that is a helpful or unhelpful thing to do. Write each one into a different square with an instruction to move forwards or backwards. For example, they might write "Take a deep breath—go forward two spaces" on one of the squares, while another might say "Hit your sister—go back five spaces."

If you are making the game towards the beginning of therapy, you might like to suggest a few options for some of the squares, commenting that you wonder whether they will be helpful or unhelpful. You might suggest that the child may want to think about these or even try these out so that you can add in next session whether these are move forward or back options.

After making the game, you can play it together as a way of reviewing the strategies.

FOR PARENTS

If parents are in the room when you make the game, try to have them contribute. What do they find helpful when they feel anxious or angry? Ask the child if that would work for them. What would be something unhelpful for the parent to do? What has the parent noticed their child doing (helpful or unhelpful)?

This is a good one to send home with the child, along with dice so they are ready to play with parents and siblings, to provide further opportunities for review and discussion.

DEVELOPMENTAL CONSIDERATIONS

If you are making a game with younger children, it will need to be simple, with fewer and larger squares to enable easier play. They may like to add pictures to the squares to represent the strategy or response. Be prepared to help with the counting and to offer suggestions of helpful and unhelpful strategies, emphasizing those that are behavioral. The Snakes and Ladders variation described below is also a simple game that many young children will be able to understand and play.

Older children tend to like games that are more complicated and may like to create cards that they have to pick up when they land on particular squares. For example, a card might say "You choose to calm down in your room, advance ten spaces" or "You remember to think 'I can do it'—move ahead five spaces." Older children may be able to generate a larger range of strategies, including cognitive and behavioral strategies.

VARIATION

You may also like to use the format of Snakes and Ladders. In this variation, we explain that ladders are helpful things that let us move forward, so in this game we think of ladders that help to manage anxiety or anger. We draw in the ladders, and write or draw the helpful strategies in the squares in which the ladders begin. We then explain that the snakes are those things that are unhelpful and draw in some snakes. We consider unhelpful things the child might do in response to their feelings, drawing or writing one near each snake's head.

To assist with generalization, you may ask parents to prompt children to consider whether something they are doing is a snake or a ladder when relevant.

Other examples of board games to make in therapy can be found online. A similar activity is also presented in Hobday and Ollier (2005), who also use a Snakes and Ladders game, though they write behaviors they want to promote on the ladders and unacceptable behaviors on the snakes.

Board game template

Body mapping

Body mapping is a child-friendly psychoeducation activity, commonly used in assisting children to better recognize and understand anxiety or anger. It is used to improve children's awareness of the physiological and cognitive aspects of emotions, to normalize these responses, and to reduce confusion or fear about these responses. It also helps to provide a rationale for emotion regulation strategies that may be taught later (for example, breathing, muscle relaxation or cognitive-change strategies). It is a component of many CBT programs, for example, the Cool Kids program (Rapee *et al.* 2006) and similar activities have been described in other books (e.g. Huebner 2005; Whitehouse and Pudney 1998). We describe here the way that we introduce and use body mapping, along with ideas and variations that we find helpful.

MATERIALS

» You will need some paper and markers.

» You may like to photocopy the *Body mapping template* on page 104 or use a cardboard cut-out of a body (both are optional).

PROCEDURE

Ask the child to draw an outline of their body on the paper (you can be drawing one yourself as a model) or use a cardboard cut-out or the template provided.

Ask the child to draw their face showing the feeling you are working on (worried/ scared/angry).

Ask the child to write down the different feelings words they use for this emotion somewhere next to the body—what do they call this feeling (for example, worried, nervous, scared, stressed)?

Ask them to remember a recent time when they were feeling the emotion that you are working on. Ask them to remember what they felt in their body and to draw or write onto their picture the different sensations they recall. You may need to prompt them to consider different body sensations, particularly those that commonly occur when people are anxious/angry. For example, "Did you notice anything about your breathing?" "Did you notice anything in your tummy?" It can be helpful to model by example, describing some of what you feel when you experience that emotion.

Depending on the child's awareness and understanding of his/her bodily changes, you may need to include some physical activities to assist in their understanding. For example:

• To help them consider muscle tightness, you can both get up and alternate making your bodies into hard/tight objects (for example, "Let's be robots/traffic lights/ brick walls") then floppy/soft objects ("Let's be jellyfish/rag dolls/spaghetti").

Alternate tight and floppy, and once they understand the idea, ask the child to make suggestions of what you can be next. Then talk with them about the difference between tight versus floppy muscles, and how their muscles feel when they are experiencing anxiety/anger versus feeling relaxed.

- To help them consider heart rate and breathing, you can bring their awareness to their breathing and heart beating while relaxed (if they can notice it!) then run on the spot for a minute or two and try again. If you have a stethoscope to use before and after, that can be helpful.

Ask the child to remember what they were thinking when they were experiencing the emotion. Prompt them to consider the type of thoughts they have when they feel this way. For example, worry thoughts often begin with "what if…," and many people think "that's not fair" when they are angry. Write the thoughts the child identifies with in thought bubbles next to the body.

Normalize the child's experiences of the emotion, using this activity as an opportunity to educate them about physiological aspects of that emotion ("the system in our body that turns on when we feel worried/angry") and the cognitive aspects ("how we start to think worry thoughts/angry thoughts"). Talk about how we can learn ways to calm down our bodies and our thoughts.

FOR PARENTS

If a parent is present in the session, they can join in and complete their own body map. If not, time should be spent in session allowing the child to tell their parent about their body map, to reinforce their learning and enhance their parents' understanding.

It is helpful if parents can reinforce this work at home when they notice their child is experiencing the emotion by saying, for example, "I can see that you are feeling worried. What are you noticing in your body right now? What thoughts are you noticing right now?"

DEVELOPMENTAL CONSIDERATIONS

This activity is appropriate and relevant for children of all ages, but should be adjusted to suit the child's own language and own level of understanding of the concepts. For younger children, the activity can be made more fun and less abstract by completing it on the floor using an outline of the child's body on a large piece of butcher's paper, or having them stick colored stickers onto the relevant parts of their bodies. Younger children will generally need more examples of physiological changes to be provided by the therapist or parent, or by looking at a simple feelings book. They are also less likely to have insight into their thoughts, but a thought bubble with a simple relevant example provided by the parent or therapist is still helpful.

VARIATIONS

This activity can be made more appealing by using a cardboard cut-out of a body which the child can glue to paper, and/or colored paper (with the color chosen by the child to represent the emotion you are working on). Alternatively, it can be completed on a whiteboard then a photo printed or emailed for the child to take home.

EXTENSION

Reading a book about the relevant emotion can help to reinforce these concepts as well as to further normalize the child's experiences of emotions. It may also help to provide some ideas if the child is feeling stuck and unsure of what changes occur for them. You can suggest that maybe they will notice one of these changes in their body the next time they are scared/angry.

Body mapping template

Bowl it over

This therapy activity is active, hands-on and uses visual cues. It was developed to assist children to articulate and appreciate situations that they find difficult and also to consider what they can do to help manage these difficulties. This activity can be used either early in therapy to identify current coping strategies or late in therapy when the child is consolidating some of the strategies they have learnt.

MATERIALS

» You will need a soft ball and something to act as bowling pins to knock down. It is helpful to have pins that you can label so choose something that you can readily put stickers or glue paper onto. A simple way to do this is to use some clear plastic cups that you can slide pieces of cardboard into as the pins, as shown in the *Bowl it over example* picture overleaf. Empty food boxes also work well.

PROCEDURE

Explain to the child that you have been wondering about the things they find hard and thinking about what helps with these. Suggest that you draw or write each of the things that bother the child and stick these each onto a pin.

Take your time doing this and then set the pins up so that the child can clearly see them. You may want to reflect on how many or how few there are.

Then suggest that you think together about what would help with those things. Beginning one at a time, ask the child to think of something that helps with one of those difficulties and, when they do, allow them to have a go at knocking it down with the ball. Parents should be included and can ask what they notice helps too.

Continue in this manner until you have knocked all the pins down.

There are lots of opportunities to talk about how one helpful thing can sometimes help with more than one of the difficulties and how sometimes you try a helpful thing and it doesn't quite work, etc.

End the game on a positive with all the pins being knocked down.

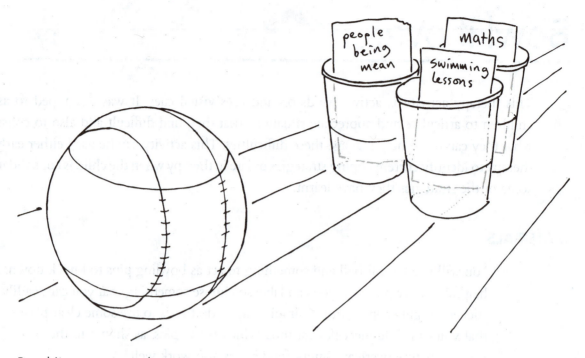

Bowl it over example

FOR PARENTS

This game should be played with parents in the room, being actively involved. Parents may also reflect on the helpful things they try and what helps them to knock down the child's difficulties.

DEVELOPMENTAL CONSIDERATIONS

Both older and younger children are likely to find this activity helpful. Focusing on behavioral strategies with younger children and including cognitive strategies with older children is a good way of making this activity developmentally appropriate.

Breaking news…

It is important in therapy for children and parents to reflect on what they have been able to achieve and any improvements they have noticed as this assists with ongoing engagement and motivation. This activity provides a fun way of reflecting on progress and small successes, and can also help children to build a picture of themselves as brave and capable.

MATERIALS

» You will need some markers and a printed television picture on an A4 page. See the *Breaking news template* provided overleaf.

» Alternatively, you could use a pretend microphone, which can sometimes be purchased in toy stores.

PROCEDURE

Ask the child if they ever watch the news. Explain to the child that you really like the good news and would love to hear all the good things that have happened in their family.

If you are making a TV, help the child to cut the screen out so you can look through it. You may like to laminate it later for durability.

Use the TV or the microphone to put on a silly voice and give headlines, like "In breaking news today Adam put his head under the water at swimming!" Take turns so that parents are also able to contribute what they have noticed.

FOR PARENTS

Some parents will find activities like this difficult and will want to bring up difficulties, by saying "Yeah, but then he…" It is important to be careful about not letting this intrude so get in quickly and reinforce for parents that this is about what is going well and that they will have plenty of time to talk about concerns later.

Families can be encouraged to take the TV home, or may borrow the microphone, so that they can reflect on the positives at the end of each day.

DEVELOPMENTAL CONSIDERATIONS

Younger children may find it difficult to recall their achievements and often need prompting from their parents in order to do so. They will, however, benefit from being prompted to consider these and from hearing their parents reflect on their achievements.

VARIATIONS

Often, once therapy has commenced, it is helpful to begin each session reflecting on achievements and what is going well generally. Sometimes you can build a tower of blocks with one for each achievement; other times you might like to put stamps on a page.

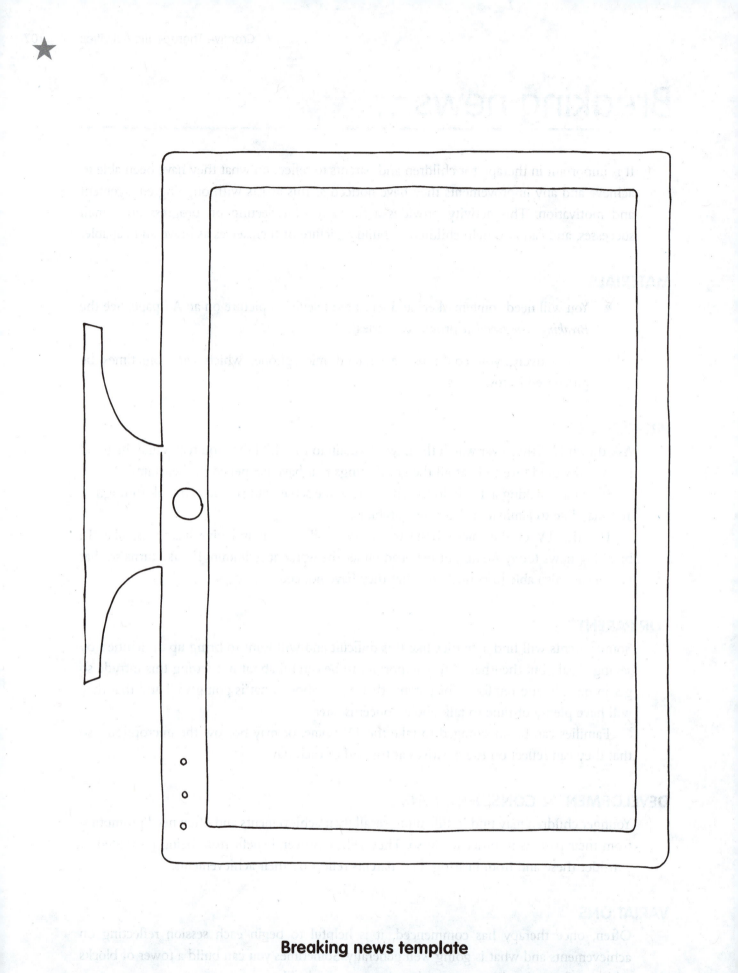

Breaking news template

Butterfly catching

Butterflies have often been used in therapy with children when creating analogies for worries, coming from the well-known expression about having "butterflies in the tummy." Young children often find it difficult to articulate their worries, and their behavioral expressions can be misinterpreted by parents. This activity helps parents and children to identify and articulate their worries. It is an active activity, involving moving about to catch butterflies, symbolizing the act of "catching" worries so that they can be observed, named and acknowledged.

MATERIALS

» You will need butterfly cut-outs. You can either cut these out freehand or if you prefer print some using the *Butterfly catching template* on page 111 and cut these out. Light (origami type) paper tends to work well as these will float a bit more easily than regular paper. Tissue paper is also a good choice if you are drawing freehand.

» You will also need markers or pencils if you choose to write the worries on the butterflies.

» Finally, you will need a small fishing net.

PROCEDURE

Explain to the child that you have noticed that they seem to feel worried sometimes and that you think this might be why they sometimes have a tummy ache, want to stay close to Mum, etc. Say that you sometimes have a wobbly tummy when you feel worried—that it almost feels as though you have butterflies in your tummy. Ask the child if they ever feel this way and say that you would like to try to catch the butterflies together.

Take turns to toss the butterflies around the room and catch them in the net. When you catch a butterfly you have to name something that makes you feel worried. If you choose to, you can write the worries on the butterflies so that you can easily reflect on these further.

FOR PARENTS

Parents can be in the room when this activity is undertaken, though if you think that the child may have worries in relation to the parent it may be best to see them alone. In these instances it would be helpful to feed back to the parent with the child and ask that they take the collage or threading home (see "Extension" section) and keep watch for any worry butterflies that are flying around at home. You may also choose to lend the child your net so that they can catch any worries that are flying around at home.

DEVELOPMENTAL CONSIDERATIONS

Younger children sometimes find it difficult to name their worries so modeling some worries or suggesting two or three worries the child may have is helpful. Having parents participating is also important as parents will be able to support this and may be able to suggest some worries they have noticed.

VARIATIONS

Liana Lowenstein has shared online her creative activity called "Butterflies in My Stomach" which, like ours, involves the use of paper butterflies in helping children to identify and verbalize their worries (also published in Lowenstein 1999). Her activity differs in that it involves gluing butterflies onto the stomach section of a body outline, and in the therapeutic conversation prompts that she suggests in order to use it as an assessment activity.

EXTENSION

Making a collage of all of the butterflies is a nice way to review the child's worries and can prompt further discussion about how she or he feels when worried and what they typically do in these circumstances. You can also thread them onto a piece of string or wool so that you can review these later.

Butterfly catching template

Calm box

The idea of using a calm box has been around for some time and is often utilized by therapists to help children (and their parents) recognize when they need to calm down and to provide tangible strategies for doing so. A similar concept has been described by others, such as Attwood's (2004) emotional toolkit, and Thomas' (2009) Coping Skills Tool Box. A calm box is a way of making emotion regulation strategies concrete for children, gathering together behavioral strategies and calming toys and activities. Where children are able to utilize cognitive strategies, they still tend to need tangible prompts initially, which can also be helpful to include in their box. What follows is our description of how we use a calm box with children.

MATERIALS

» A box; shoeboxes are a good size for younger children.

» Cardboard for creating cards.

» Photos.

» Small toys and favorite items.

» Bubbles, windmill or something else that requires the child to breathe out.

PROCEDURE

Talk with the child and parents about the notion of having a box of things that will help them to calm down.

Utilize any existing strategies and pop these into the box. For example, if a child finds a hug helpful then put in a photo of them hugging their mother or father.

Use cards to incorporate any strategies you have been discussing in therapy, such as helpful thoughts.

Include some of the child's favorite things, like a toy car or a small box of LEGO®.

Include any calming activities or sensory toys, such as a waterwheel or a stress ball.

If you have been working on breathing in therapy, try to include something that prompts the child to use this strategy, like a small container of bubbles.

FOR PARENTS

Parents should be encouraged to think about when they might use a calm box. In doing so they will be identifying high-risk times and can begin planning more carefully for these. They should also be involved in helping to talk about what calms their child, beginning with what they already know works and extending this out to include new strategies.

Many parents respond to their child's anxiety or anger by becoming anxious or angry themselves. Having a calm box gives them something to do, which is usually helpful. It also provides an avenue for thinking and talking about how they manage their emotions. What do they do to stay calm? What are the tricks in *their* calm box? Do they need help to remember how to use them?

DEVELOPMENTAL CONSIDERATIONS

A collection of hands-on calming strategies, like the *Calm box example* overleaf, is particularly useful for younger children who often otherwise struggle to think of strategies when they are upset. Older children often find a calm box helpful too, though they benefit from the inclusion of visual cues that remind them of more complex strategies, such as helpful thoughts or visual images they find calming. When using this strategy with older children, we are mindful of finding ways in which they can use their box discreetly in the broader range of settings they find themselves in, such as at school or at friends' houses, and often opt for one of the variations listed below. If parents of older children notice their child needing to calm down, after acknowledging their child's feelings they could gently prompt their child with "What can you do to help yourself feel better?" or "Is there anything in your calm box that might be helpful?"—thus encouraging their child to take the initiative in choosing and implementing strategies.

VARIATIONS

It is helpful to use language that works that works for the child and the family. For example, if they tend to talk about cooling down rather than calming down then make a cool-down box. If the child has a particular interest that you can tailor this to, such as superheroes, then think about doing so, for example, making a superpowers box.

Older children may prefer a smaller cardboard box, such as a noodle box or even a matchbox, containing cards to prompt them to use strategies learnt in therapy or other coping strategies they find helpful. Alternatives to a box include using a door hanger or paper fan (to "cool off") with written prompts for strategies, a paper bag as their "bag of tricks" or a cardboard shield with strategies represented as "badges."

EXTENSION

To assist with generalization outside of the house and clinic room, you can also work with children to develop a box for preschool or a portable little kit that they can take with them when they are out. For older children, small cards on a lanyard or reminders of their strategies on a keyring may be more appealing.

Calm box example

Colored glasses

Therapists working within a CBT framework often talk with children about helpful as opposed to unhelpful thoughts in regard to managing their feelings, and some use the metaphor of "negative glasses" to describe the unhelpful thinking pattern of focusing only on the negative aspects of a situation (Stallard 2002). This hands-on activity draws on the common saying about rose-colored glasses to demonstrate to children the role of thoughts in influencing their feelings and behavior.

MATERIALS

» You will need some cardboard glasses cut-outs. You can buy these already made or make your own using the *Colored glasses template* on page 117.

» You will also need some small pieces of cellophane in red and any other colors that you choose.

» Finally, you will need glue or tape to stick the cellophane to the glasses.

PROCEDURE

Explain to the child that there is a funny old saying about wearing rose-colored glasses. Talk about how this means seeing everything in a good way. Suggest that you make some rose-colored glasses from the cut-outs and cellophane and try them out.

Using the glasses, act out situations that the child might encounter (for example, not getting to do sport at school, missing out on an invite to someone's party, or being given some difficult homework) and take it in turns to use the rose-colored glasses, modeling a helpful or positive thought about the situation. Have the person who is role-playing reflect on how they feel in each instance.

Explain that it is hard to always be positive and that everyone sometimes sees things in an unhelpful or negative way. Suggest that you make some different colored glasses and see things in a negative way, role-playing and reflecting on how this feels as above.

Ask the child about their experience with the different colored glasses. For example, you might ask:

• Which ones did they prefer?

• How did the glasses make them feel?

• Which ones were more helpful?

• Are there times when they tend to wear unhelpful or helpful glasses?

FOR PARENTS

Parents can have a turn in the session if they are in the room. Otherwise it is helpful to introduce the glasses to them, allowing the child to model the way in which they work towards the end of the session. Agree upon something that the child could do at home with the glasses. Could everyone in the family take a turn of wearing them for an hour over the weekend? Could Dad be given them when he gets home from work to make him less grumpy?

DEVELOPMENTAL CONSIDERATIONS

The notion of helpful as opposed to unhelpful thoughts is often too complex for younger children and, as such, this activity is more appropriate for older children.

EXTENSION

Sometimes older children are able to work on realistic thinking, in which case you may like to create rose-colored glasses, a dark color for unhelpful thinking, and a more neutral color for realistic thinking. Alternatively, the child might like to put the rose-colored and dark-colored glasses on at the same time to practice realistic thinking.

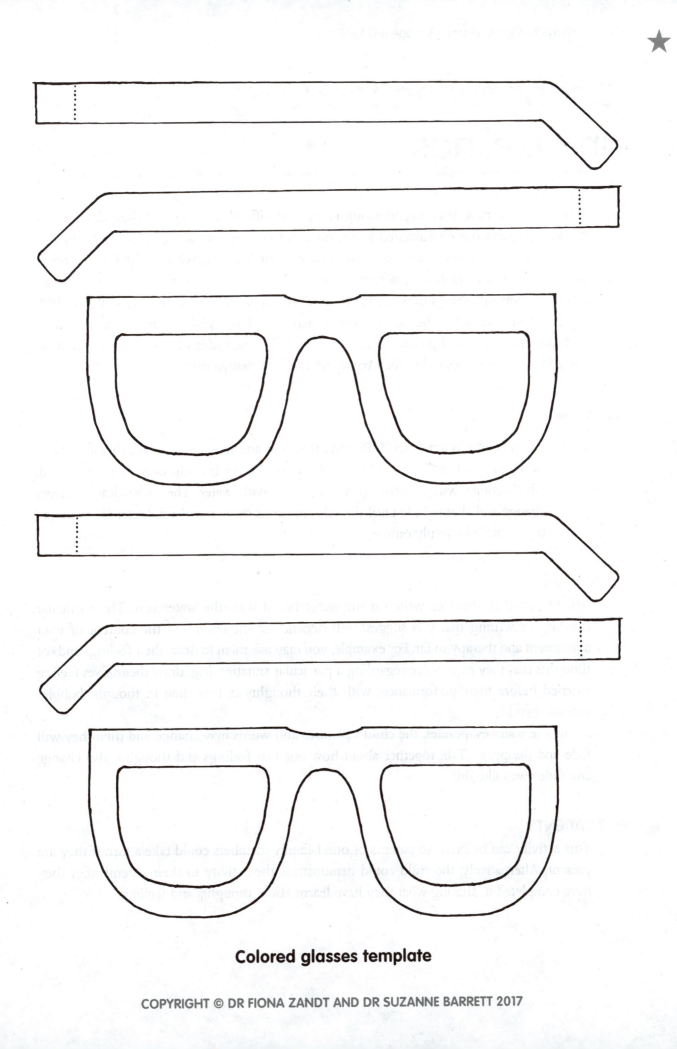

Colored glasses template

Disappearing thoughts and feelings

When children have been experiencing emotional difficulties, they and their families can become very anxious or frustrated in response to that emotion, and can react in unhelpful ways in an attempt to avoid or stop the emotion. Furthermore, when a child is distressed, they often feel as though the emotion will last forever and that the distressing thoughts are facts that they will always think and believe. This activity requires a commercially available toy, the Water Wizard or the Aquadoodle, which is used to explain to children that feelings and thoughts come and go and to explore the ACT-based idea of noticing and allowing these inner experiences rather than trying to avoid or change them.

MATERIALS

> » You'll need a Water Wizard, Buddha Board or another similar board that uses water as its ink, such as an Aquadoodle. A Water Wizard is a flip-open drawing board, which comes with a soft-tipped pen to fill with water. The water-drawn images change and slowly fade until they disappear as the water dries. Water Wizards can be purchased cheaply online.

PROCEDURE

Ask the child to draw or write on the water board with the water pen. The particular drawing or writing that you suggest will depend on the child and the content of your assessment and therapy so far. For example, you may ask them to draw their feelings and/or thoughts that they experience regarding a particular situation (e.g. draw themselves feeling worried before their performance, with their thoughts at that time in thought bubbles around them).

As the water evaporates, the child's pictures and words may change and then they will fade and disappear. Talk together about how our real feelings and thoughts also change and fade away like this.

FOR PARENTS

This activity can be brief, so parents or other family members could take a turn if they are present. Alternatively, the child could demonstrate the activity to their parents after they have completed it, sharing what they have learnt about thoughts and feelings.

DEVELOPMENTAL CONSIDERATIONS

Both younger and older children benefit from learning that feelings come and go and both are likely to enjoy this activity. Older children will be able to talk more about how thoughts also come and go; however, for younger children it is generally easier to focus on feelings when completing this activity.

VARIATION

The water board can also be useful in helping anxious and reluctant children to share their thoughts, feelings, ideas or experiences through writing or drawing, as it is not permanent and is appealing to many children.

EXTENSION

This activity is also helpful when introducing and teaching mindfulness to children, as the water board drawing involves focusing on the present moment and the concepts explored encourage awareness of changing feelings and thoughts.

Family feelings inventory

This activity provides a visual means for family members to communicate how they are each feeling and, in doing so, aims to enhance family members' awareness of each other's emotions as well as of their own emotions. It increases the extent to which emotions are recognized and labeled within the home and fosters further discussion about feelings.

MATERIALS

» You will need a whiteboard and whiteboard markers.

PROCEDURE

You can introduce this activity by explaining that families differ greatly in the extent to which they talk about feelings. You can then explain that you would like to do a bit of an inventory about how they are all feeling at the moment.

Using a whiteboard draw a face for each person in the family and write their name beside it. Then ask all of the family members who are present to find a word to describe how they feel at that moment, and depict this feeling on their face. You can ask others in the room about whether they could see any clues that would have enabled them to identify that feeling. For example, can they tell that someone is happy because their eyes are shiny or that someone is excited because they are having trouble sitting still?

For family members who aren't there, ask those who are to guess how they are feeling. Sometimes children will respond by saying that they can't guess, which provides a good opportunity to explain that we guess about the feelings of others all the time. Indeed, it would be very difficult to function in our world if we did not. It's a good opportunity to talk about what clues you might use when guessing about others—such as thinking about what they like and what they are likely to think about a particular situation.

Once you have all the family members' faces depicting their feelings you can talk about whether or not it is helpful to know how everyone is feeling. You may like to ask the child some questions about how they would like their mother to be feeling if they were intending to ask for an ice-cream and other examples.

You can talk with the family about whether it would be helpful to have a space in the house where everyone could draw how they are feeling. Talk about where this physical space would be and when people would record this; for example, would it be when they first wake up in the morning? Or when they get home?

FOR PARENTS

Parents may feel like the idea of a whiteboard at home won't work for them, in which case you may wish to encourage them to ask each person how they are feeling at dinner time, if the family eats dinner together. If not, try to talk with the family about alternatives that might work for them. Remember that the family does not need to do this in an ongoing way. Treating it as a one week experiment is often helpful and may enable the family to attempt it.

DEVELOPMENTAL CONSIDERATIONS

Most younger children will be able to identify their feelings and, as such, can participate in this activity. Their ability to consider the feelings of others may be limited, though the activity may assist in increasing this. The activity is also helpful for older children.

VARIATIONS

Another alternative is to do this at the beginning of each session with the family, reflecting that it is helpful to know how everyone is feeling before starting the session.

Family feelings jump

This is an active feelings game to play with the whole family or a subset of the family. The objective is to help families appreciate that individuals within the family often feel differently about the same thing. It helps parents and children to consider their own feelings as well as to see each other's perspectives, which is important in relating well as a family.

MATERIALS

» You will need to either draw some feelings pictures with the child or you may like to use enlarged copies of the *Feelings faces template* (see the *Feeling block people* activity for the template), some scissors to cut them out and some blu-tak (poster putty) or tape to stick the pictures on the discs.

» You can stick the feelings pictures on discs, large sheets of card or small carpet squares.

PROCEDURE

Begin by asking the child/children about some of their feelings and as you do this, set up the activity by placing feelings pictures around the floor. Explain that you want to know more about how different people in the family feel and will be asking each of them to jump on the feelings face that describes how they feel in a given situation.

Begin with some simple situations, such as having ice-cream for dessert. Move up to ones that are more complex and likely to elicit different feelings, such as running late for school. If people are unable to decide on any one feeling, they can jump from one to another to represent that they feel both or can put one leg on each or similar. Sometimes the chaos this causes is a good opportunity to reflect on how many different feelings there are and how this can be very confusing.

Once they are warmed up, try to use some situations that are of particular relevance for the family. Ask the parents whether they knew that their child felt a particular way and foster some moments of connection.

FOR PARENTS

This is a great activity for talking about the importance of empathizing. It is helpful to talk about how parents can reflect and acknowledge their child's emotions during difficult moments, while maintaining an awareness of their own.

DEVELOPMENTAL CONSIDERATIONS

This activity is enjoyable for both older and younger children as it involves getting up and moving about. Younger children are generally able to reflect on how they feel in a particular situation, especially with the support of visual cues, which the activity provides. They may, however, struggle to appreciate that people feel differently about the same situation. Often, though, we use this activity to help parents see a situation from their child's perspective and find that young children enjoy the activity and benefit from the opportunity to express their feelings.

Fear hierarchy

Developing a fear hierarchy to assist with exposure is a core component of CBT for phobias and other anxiety disorders. These are used to help children and parents identify small steps which they can use to gradually face their fears, and to pay attention to small successes along the way. Variations can be found in many programs. For example, the Cool Kids program uses a stepladder analogy to develop "Step-by-Step Plans" (Rapee *et al.* 2006), the Friends program uses a staircase analogy to develop "Step Plans" (Barrett 1999), and Stallard (2002) similarly uses a ladder. What follows is a description of the way we use fear hierarchies with children.

MATERIALS

> » You will need paper and markers. Sometimes a big long roll of paper can be fun to use for this, or poster-sized paper.

> » A *Fear hierarchy template* is provided on page 126, which can be photocopied.

PROCEDURE

Talk with the parents and the child about the importance of exposure—that we need to face our fears to beat our fears. The more we avoid something, the more afraid of it we become. On the other hand, the more times we do something, the less scary it becomes, until it is not scary at all. See if you can find an example of something the child used to be nervous about, but no longer is due to exposure or practice (e.g. they may have been anxious the first time they went to swimming, or school, or came to see you).

Talk with the parents and the child about what is the most scary thing they want to learn how to manage and write this down on the paper.

Ask about any smaller steps they can think of and have the child let you know where they would like to put these. It is important that the first step is achievable, and that steps are not too big. It is helpful for steps to also be clear and specific, and something that can be practiced easily and frequently.

You will most likely have to work together with the child and parent to identify some of the steps. It is also helpful to consider the hierarchy a rough plan and let the family know that you can move, add or take out steps as you go along.

Try to come up with an interesting format that suits the child and family. It might be a staircase or ladder to success, or a tree with lots of branches at varying heights, or steps along the way, for which you could trace the child's foot. Children who like computer games may like to think about game levels.

While the full hierarchy may be drawn to demonstrate the concept, for some children, it may be best to initially leave the higher steps blank, with only the first, very small step filled in (though it often helps if they have articulated the overall goal they are working towards). Explain that we will be facing this fear gradually, a little step at a time, and they will have help along the way. This approach can be helpful for children who may become overwhelmed by considering all the steps at the start, contributing to their avoidance of even the first step. In this case, as the child masters steps, the next steps can be added in, until they gain confidence in their ability to climb them all.

It is helpful to discuss rewarding the child for trying as well as for succeeding in taking each step. How could the child reward him/herself? How could the family reward the child? You may even like to develop a "reward menu" together with the child and parent to assist in motivating the child and in drawing the family's attention to efforts and small successes. The rewards can be small and need to be practical so that the family are easily able to follow through with them. For this reason, a parent needs to be involved in this discussion.

It is also helpful to discuss what tools the child and family have that they will use to help them take the first step, to reinforce the idea of using the anxiety-management strategies they have learnt.

FOR PARENTS

Sometimes the child's avoidance means they are reluctant to complete a fear hierarchy and it is best to do this with parents alone. It is often helpful to talk with parents about how this is a good model for helping their child manage their fears and think about how it could be adapted to other situations.

DEVELOPMENTAL CONSIDERATIONS

This activity is helpful and appropriate for children of all ages. For younger children, the involvement of their parents is essential, both in developing the fear hierarchy and in supporting their child to implement each step.

My Goal

_____

_____

_____

_____

_____

_____

_____

_____

_____

_____

_____

_____

_____

_____

_____

_____

Fear hierarchy template

Feeling block people

Young children can find it hard to talk about feelings and often benefit from doing so in play. This activity involves making people from wooden blocks and feelings faces. It is designed to elicit play with the child and, within that play, reflection on feelings.

MATERIALS

» You will need some plain wooden blocks.

» You will also need some feeling faces (see *Feeling faces template* on page 129), some scissors to cut them out and some blu-tack (poster putty) or tape to stick the faces on the blocks.

» You may also like to use some markers or pencils to color the faces in.

PROCEDURE

Explain to the child that you thought you could make some dolls (out of the blocks) today. Say that you have some faces that you can use to stick on the dolls.

Allow the child to choose a face for the first doll and see if they can name the feeling they have chosen. You can ask:

• What made the doll feel that way?

• What sorts of things make you feel that way?

• Tell me about a time you felt that way?

Continue doing this until you have a few emotions covered, trying to include some positive as well as some negative emotions.

You may then wish to engage the child in some play using the dolls.

FOR PARENTS

Ideally you send the block people home with the child, in which case they may like to decorate the blocks with markers or paint. Parents can be encouraged to play with the child and use this as a way to begin talking more about feelings.

DEVELOPMENTAL CONSIDERATIONS

This activity is particularly appealing to younger children, who should readily use it to engage in some discussion around feelings. It may also be useful with some older children, particularly those who are more resistant to talking about their feelings.

EXTENSION

Children often like to do this with family photos and this often leads to some interesting play. You can link the two activities by having children add feeling faces in as well, with this providing a nice way of reflecting on the fact that feelings change.

Feeling faces template

Feeling bubbles

Children's heightened emotions are often accompanied by the child and parents experiencing anxiety about the emotion itself and a pressure to fix or get rid of the emotion. This can cause more anxiety or frustration, and children can feel overwhelmed and stuck in the emotion. This activity provides a simple way of helping children learn that feelings come and go, and that they can notice and acknowledge their emotions which will in time pass without them needing to do anything to change them, consistent with an ACT framework.

MATERIALS

> » All that is required for this activity is a bottle of bubbles. We like to have a good quality bubble mixture that blows a lot of bubbles in one go. We tend to blow the bubbles; however, you could also use a bubble machine for this.

PROCEDURE

Begin by explaining to the child that you were thinking about their feelings and thought in some ways they were a bit like bubbles. The child will generally ask what you mean at this point which enables you to offer to show them.

You can then blow some bubbles, commenting as you do that you noticed that some of the child's feelings were big and some were small, some were happy and some were sad, etc. You can then comment that another thing that reminded you of the bubbles is that the child's feelings come and go—they don't last forever.

Tell the child that you will test this out together and say that you will blow some happy feelings and see if they can make the feelings (as symbolized by the bubbles) last forever. Ask the child what makes them feel happy and then blow some happy feelings asking the child to do whatever they can to stop them from popping. Have fun with this, encouraging the child to catch them in their hands or try having a bubble land on their head. Comment as you watch the bubbles on how some last longer than others and reflect when the bubbles stop about times when you have felt happy, either briefly or for a longer time.

You can repeat this process with other feelings, such as anger, sadness or worry. You may find that the child wants to pop these bubbles quickly. It is helpful to respond by allowing the child to do so and commenting on the discomfort these feelings cause them rather than trying to control this too much.

FOR PARENTS

If you have parents in the room you can ask for some of their feelings too when you are blowing bubbles. Parents often find it reassuring to consider how all feelings are normal and passing, and that they can empathize and allow their child to experience the emotion, rather than needing to fix it. Some parents have found it helpful to remind their children at home that their feelings are like bubbles and will come and go.

DEVELOPMENTAL CONSIDERATIONS

This is a simple activity that appeals to younger children in particular. Many older children will also enjoy this activity though if they do feel uncomfortable about using bubbles *Disappearing thoughts and feelings* may be a more appropriate activity for them.

EXTENSION

These concepts can be further explored and experienced through many mindfulness practices. Ideas and resources for practicing mindfulness with children were discussed in Chapter 6.

Feelings buzzer

Children benefit from being able to recognize and name their emotions and this is very much a prerequisite to being able to successfully implement strategies for managing emotions. This activity provides a fun way to practice noticing the bodily sensations that accompany changes in emotions and naming current feelings. Completing this activity when children have done some work on emotions helps with generalizing these skills to home and school. When completed with parents in the room it supports parents to tune in to their child's emotions and to assist with generalization.

MATERIALS

» You will need something for a buzzer. This can be a round laminated circle or a piece of craft foam cut in the shape of a buzzer. Another alternative is to use a bell, though some children may become more focused on ringing this than on completing the activity.

PROCEDURE

Explain to the child that you think they have done a good job of learning about their feelings and how their body changes when they have these feelings. Talk with the child about how sometimes these changes can be hard to notice when you are busy playing at home or at school. Suggest that you practice noticing any changes while you are playing today by using a buzzer. Explain that if anyone notices any changes in their feelings or anyone else's they should hit the buzzer. Go on to make the buzzer if you are intending to do so during the session or introduce the buzzer that you have, allowing the child to try it out. Make a silly buzz or beep sound when you hit the buzzer and have the child practice this too.

Leave the buzzer somewhere prominent and engage the child in playing a game or similar. Board games are often good here as the experience of winning and losing evokes emotions. When the child hits the buzzer have them explain what they noticed and think of a feeling word to describe it. For example, a child may feel excited and smile and raise their arms if they win. You can hit the buzzer if the child doesn't and ask that the child look closely and notice what is going on inside of them or for someone else.

The child may like to take the buzzer home and see what they notice changing at home too.

FOR PARENTS

Parents can readily be included in this activity and it is often helpful to do so if you are concerned about their ability to read their child's feelings. If they are not present then have the child show them the buzzer afterwards and explain some of what they noticed. If the family are taking the buzzer home, talk with them about when it might be most helpful and who tends to be best at noticing changes.

This activity is also a helpful lead in for parents who tend to respond by altering the situation to avoid escalating their child's feelings. You can talk with them about the importance of children being able to recognize and label their own feelings and talk about how they can be a buzzer, facilitating the child's development in this regard.

DEVELOPMENTAL CONSIDERATIONS

Both older and younger children will enjoy this activity. Younger children will benefit from having their parents in the room to assist them to identify their emotions.

Feelings in our family

This activity was developed for use with families, to help parents and children appreciate that the emotions of one family member can affect the whole family, sometimes in different ways. This can be particularly helpful for allowing parents to consider the impact their own feelings may have.

MATERIALS

>> You will need a ball of wool or some string and some scissors.

PROCEDURE

Explain to the family that one thing you know about families is that everyone in a family is connected. Say that because of this you thought it might be helpful to play a game that may help you to learn about how these connections work in their family.

Explain that the connections between family members can't be seen so you have brought in some wool so that you will be able to see them while you play. Ask if it is okay for you to link the family together with the wool and if they agree begin to gently tie the wool around each person so the family is linked.

Begin simply by telling the family that you would like to experiment to see what happens when something happens to one person in the family. If the family are sitting, have one person stand, or if they are standing, ask someone to sit. Reflect upon the impact this has on the others before trying another simple one, like having someone jump or jog on the spot.

Once you have tried a few examples untie the string and explain to the family that it is often their emotions that will affect each other the most. Ask one of the parents to talk about what they notice when they are feeling angry or worried. What do they do and who does it affect the most? Tie the string around the parents and then link it to the person they feel it affects the most, repeating the process so that you are able to see how all family members are affected. You should end up with a great big messy tangle. You can then cut the family out of the wool.

If the child is comfortable doing so, they may like to talk about their difficulties, repeating the process so that you can demonstrate the way in which this impacts on all the family members as above.

FOR PARENTS

It is important for parents to be actively involved in this activity, reflecting on the impact that their own feelings may have on others in the family, as well as how they respond emotionally to others' feelings.

DEVELOPMENTAL CONSIDERATIONS

Younger and older children will enjoy participating in this activity and the core concept (i.e. that we are all connected) is one that young children can grasp when it is presented in this practical manner. Children are generally happy to participate in this activity and even if their understanding of the core concept remains simplistic, this is rarely a cause for concern as most of the time it is the parents whose ideas we are most hoping to influence.

EXTENSION

Prior to cutting the family out of the wool, you can explain that families often find themselves in this sort of tangle and that there are ways to make this easier. Help the family to generate ideas that might make the situation easier, cutting the wool for each idea they come up with.

Feelings juggle

Children benefit from a greater awareness and understanding of their emotions, and this activity helps them to realize that they can have a range of different feelings about an experience. Understanding these complexities about their emotions and experiences, including both positive and negative aspects, can help them to develop a more balanced viewpoint and realistic understanding.

MATERIALS

» You will need some small balls for juggling. You can cheaply purchase some juggling balls, though any small balls will do.

PROCEDURE

Ask the child if they can juggle and explain that sometimes you feel like you are juggling a whole lot of different feelings. Ask them to hold on to the balls while you show them what you mean.

Think of an example that is relevant to the child. For example, you could say that you were at the show with your friend and were happy to be there. You can ask the child to throw you a ball to symbolize your happy feelings. You can then add another element to the scenario. For example, you could say that your friend wanted to go on a ride; however, you thought the ride was too high up and so you felt a little scared. As you say this ask the child to throw you another ball for scared and begin juggling. You could then mention that you also felt worried that your friend would ask you to go on the ride with them and ask the child to throw you another juggling ball. Try to juggle these feelings and reflect on how it is becoming more difficult. Finally if you haven't already dropped your juggling balls you could add another element to the scenario, explaining that you felt embarrassed about needing to tell your friend that you were scared of the ride and ask the child to throw you a final ball. You don't need to have great juggling skills for this activity. In fact, it helps if you don't as you can comment on how much harder it is with all those feelings.

You can then ask the child to think of a situation in which they experienced a number of feelings or, if it is more manageable for the child, give them an example and toss them feelings as you talk through what they experience (as in the above example).

FOR PARENTS

This is a good one to demonstrate for parents if they have not been in the room for the activity. It is worth explaining to them that it is helpful for children to realize that they can experience a range of feelings about the same situation. Being able to reflect on positive and negative aspects of the situation is helpful for children as it enables them to have a more balanced perspective and can support more creative problem solving.

DEVELOPMENTAL CONSIDERATIONS

Younger children often have difficulties understanding mixed emotions but do experience them. If using this activity with younger children, use simple examples and fewer emotions— even just two. It is important to involve their parent in the session, as the greatest gains may come from the parent gaining insight and being able to name the child's different emotions in the moment when they experience them. Most older children will readily understand and enjoy this activity.

Feelings that show

Children often express anxiety, sadness or disappointment through anger. When parents are able to identify the emotions that underlie their child's anger, they are often better able to empathize with their child and respond in a more supportive way. Older children themselves benefit from gaining awareness and understanding of their emotions that trigger their anger, and this may also allow them to articulate those feelings.

MATERIALS

> » You will need a cardboard tube, such as a toilet paper or paper towel roll. You will also need some markers, scissors and cardboard or paper.

PROCEDURE

Begin by explaining to the child that you would like to make a toy to help you think more about what is happening when they get angry. Have them draw themselves feeling angry on the tube. Use this opportunity to talk about what makes them feel angry and how they experience it in their body.

Begin talking about how sometimes there are other feelings that can be hiding underneath anger and suggest some that may be relevant, such as sadness, disappointment or jealousy. If the child or parent identifies that one of these feelings may be underneath their anger then write that feeling down or draw a picture of that emotion on the cardboard and hide it in the tube. You should be able to slide it in so that it remains hidden without needing tape. Depending on the child there may be a number of feelings that you hide inside the tube.

Older children can also be engaged in some discussion about how things might be different if they showed one of their hidden feelings rather than their anger. They can be asked, for example, how their parents, teachers or friends might respond and to think about whether that would be better or worse for them.

FOR PARENTS

If parents are not in the room when you complete this activity then engage them in some discussion afterwards. Ask about whether they knew that some of those feelings were hiding under there. Wonder whether they have the same experience at times. Ask how they would respond differently if the child were to show one of their hidden feelings rather than anger.

This activity leads nicely to talking with families about how they can respond when their child is angry. Helping parents to think about the underlying emotion is often very helpful.

DEVELOPMENTAL CONSIDERATIONS

Most older children will readily understand and benefit from this activity. Younger children may enjoy the craft activity, though are likely to find the concept very difficult to understand and generalize. Younger children will need their parents involved in the session to assist, and it is the parent's increased insight that is most likely to be most therapeutic. Parents may be able to provide their younger children with language for those emotions in the moment that are otherwise masked by the anger.

Feelings thermometer

A feelings thermometer or scale is a widely used visual scaling technique, used to assist children in recognizing the different intensities or levels of an emotion. In doing so, it helps children and their parents to notice when they are starting to become anxious or angry, providing an opportunity to implement strategies before the feelings escalate and become more difficult to manage. It is used in a number of CBT approaches to childhood anxiety and anger, such as the Cool Kids program (Rapee *et al.* 2006) and Stallard's (2002) Think Good—Feel Good. Some variations published by other authors are listed below. We have presented here a description of the way that we introduce and use this common and helpful intervention with children.

MATERIALS

» You will need a printed picture of a thermometer or scale rated 0–10. A *Feelings thermometer template* is provided on page 142 or you may prefer to hand-draw the scale.

» You will also need colored pencils or markers.

PROCEDURE

Talk with the child about how an actual thermometer works, for example if placed in cool water which is then heated up to boil. Depending on the child's interests and understanding of this, you may instead use a computer game analogy, and talk about the different levels of the computer game (which has no "cheats" to skip levels), or the levels of an elevator. It is helpful if they understand that levels on the scale cannot get skipped over (though sometimes they pass very quickly).

Together with the child, add some words to the thermometer, chosen by the child to describe low levels (e.g. 0 = calm/cool; 2 = okay/bit annoyed); medium levels (4 = more annoyed/sort of angry; 6 = angry); and high levels (8 = very angry; 10 = extremely furious). They may also like to draw faces to depict the different levels of feelings. It is not necessary to label every level—labeling every second level is sufficient. You may like to talk with the child about recent experiences and what thermometer rating they would have been at.

Ask the child to color the bottom third in a calm color, the middle third a "medium" color, and the top third a very angry/anxious color.

Talk to the child about how easy/hard it is for them to calm down at the different levels of the thermometer and, given that, where on the thermometer is the best place for them to use their strategies to calm down (this should be somewhere around the middle third).

Discuss how they feel at that level on the thermometer—what they have noticed in their body, thoughts, feelings and behavior.

Reinforce these concepts at future sessions when discussing how the child is feeling in session, or how they were feeling during recent experiences, by asking them to rate their feelings on the thermometer. Thermometer ratings may also be used if you are giving monitoring tasks for homework.

FOR PARENTS

Provide feedback to the parent about the activity, together with the child. Prompt the child to tell his/her parent about the thermometer, what they have learnt, and how they plan to use it.

Parents can be encouraged to use the thermometer in talking to their child about their feelings, particularly when they are experiencing any anger/anxiety, to prompt their child to consider what level his/her feelings are at. For example, a parent may be able to say, "I can see that you are feeling worried; how high are you on the worry thermometer right now?" The thermometer can be brought home by the child as a visual prompt for these conversations.

Some parents may also consider modeling its use for themselves, when appropriate. They may say, for example, "I'm feeling frustrated, I'm at about 4 on the thermometer, which is in the orange, so I'm going to take a break to calm myself down."

DEVELOPMENTAL CONSIDERATIONS

This activity as described here is best suited to older children. Depending on developmental level and the child's experience of emotions, a scale with five levels may be simpler and more appropriate.

If using this activity with younger children, a simple scale is often more helpful than introducing the thermometer concept. A three-level scale is generally most helpful, though some children may manage a five-level scale. Pictures alongside the scale depicting the different intensities are also important, such as feelings faces or another analogy relevant to the child (e.g. dinosaurs of increasing size, or volcanos progressing from calm to erupting).

VARIATIONS

It is important to use language that works for the child and the family (e.g. calling it a worry game or a fear scale rather than an anxiety thermometer). Using the child's own language or an analogy they are familiar with is ideal.

Some variations published previously have been Huebner's (2007a) "fear measuring stick," Romain and Verdick's (2000) "stress-o-meter" and Wever and Phillips' (1996) "wobbly thermometer" (measuring the "School Wobblies"). Buron and Curtis (2013) present many variations and uses for their "Incredible 5-Point Scale."

Feelings thermometer template

Helpful thought bracelet

This is a useful and often appealing activity which provides a portable visual reminder for children of a helpful thought that assists them when they feel worried, angry or sad. This activity is best used once the child has learnt about helpful and unhelpful thoughts, to assist them in using cognitive strategies in their homes or schools.

MATERIALS

» You will need some letter beads as well as some plain (or spacer) beads and something to thread them on, such as cord or thread. If you are using thread, a needle is helpful. Beads are readily available from craft stores or online.

PROCEDURE

Explain that you have been impressed by all of what the child has learnt about helpful thoughts. Say that managing unhelpful thoughts can be easy in sessions but coming up with helpful thoughts at school or at home can be really hard. Suggest that you make a bracelet with a thought that will help the child remember what to do when they feel worried, angry or sad.

Explain that the child can use the letters to spell out a helpful thought or key words that will remind them of that thought. You may want to give them some examples, such as "I can do this" or "My family is okay"

Help the child to make the bracelet by threading the beads and engage them in conversation while doing so.

Some questions that you might like to ask include:

• What made you choose that thought?

• Can you think of a time when that thought has worked for you?

• What is it about that thought that is helpful?

• When do you think you will most need your bracelet?

• Are there times when it will be hard to do what the bracelet says?

• What will you do in those situations?

FOR PARENTS

Encourage the child to show their bracelet to their parents and explain when they think they will use it. Ask the child whether they would like their parents to remind them to look at their bracelet if they notice that they are becoming upset. If so, ask the child what the best way for parents to remind them is. Children sometimes like to come up with secret signals for their parents to use.

It can be helpful to ask parents what a thought is that they find particularly helpful, one *they* would put on a bracelet if they were making one.

DEVELOPMENTAL CONSIDERATIONS

Both older and younger children are likely to find this activity useful. If you are using this with younger children try to come up with a simple thought that can be used across a range of situations. Older children may prefer to generate a thought that relates more to the particular difficulty they are struggling with. Using larger beads is preferable for younger children while older children tend to like smaller beads. Ensure that you do not use beads with children who may swallow them, as they represent a choking hazard.

VARIATION

Instead of a bracelet, the child might prefer a necklace like the one shown in the *Helpful thought bracelet example* below or a keyring, made by threading the beads onto wire or cord then connecting it to an empty keyring.

In the process of writing this book we read Thomas' (2009) book on developing coping skills in children. Thomas uses a number of bracelets to help children remember coping strategies and to remind them of what is important to them.

Helpful thought bracelet example

In my heart

This activity provides an opportunity to explore with children their passions and developing priorities. For therapists familiar with ACT, this can be conceptualized as helping children to discover what is important to them or what really matters to them. It can help to promote resilience by helping children to identify their strengths and resources and to develop a positive self-concept. For some children, it may also be helpful in identifying goals and providing motivation for change.

MATERIALS

» You will need paper or cardboard in two different colors, markers and scissors.

» You will be making and decorating a heart-shaped envelope, so you will also need tape, glue or a stapler. Alternatively, you may prefer to use a ready-made heart-shaped craft box, or another small box on which you draw a large heart.

PROCEDURE

Explain to the child that you would like to explore what things are really important to them, and suggest that you make a heart-shaped envelope (or use the heart-shaped box) to fill with those important things. Explain that there are no right or wrong answers, that we all have different things that we consider important, and that is okay.

Use cards or squares of paper for the child to write, or draw, those things of high importance to them. Some older children may like to have two different size squares, or two different colors of paper, to differentiate things that are very important from those that are of medium importance.

Prompt the child with examples that they may consider whether or not to include, such as the following:

- passions or special interests, such as extra-curricular activities or hobbies they really enjoy

- people or relationships such as parents, siblings, extended family members, teachers, friends or others

- learning or school-based activities

- being healthy or more specific healthy behaviors such as being active, having down-time or eating well

- community involvement or religion

- social behaviors, such as being kind, generous or honest, helping others or socializing

- more general behaviors or activities, such as having fun, playing or trying new things.

It is helpful for the child to take their craft heart home with them, and you may like to talk with the child about who they might show it to and where they will keep it.

FOR PARENTS

If this activity is completed with a child alone, the child may then be happy to share with the parent what they have created and considered. Alternatively, parents can be involved in this activity by completing their own craft heart at the same time, as they may find it helpful to explore their own values and priorities, and reflect (without judgment) on points of similarity and difference with their child's.

DEVELOPMENTAL CONSIDERATIONS

This activity is most helpful and relevant for older children who are better able to begin to reflect on and develop an understanding of what really matters to them. Those in upper primary school may like to differentiate between different levels of importance. For others, just identifying whether things are important or not is sufficient. If used with younger children, the focus should be on what they enjoy and feel good about. Depending on their reading level, pictures may be helpful alongside or instead of the words.

Kick-back soccer

Anxiety and mood difficulties are often associated with unhelpful or negative thoughts and many CBT programs incorporate strategies to manage these thoughts, such as answering back with a more helpful thought. This is an active, out of chair activity, with a practical sports analogy, that was developed to demonstrate and practice the concept of countering unhelpful thoughts.

MATERIALS

> » You will need a soft ball.

PROCEDURE

Toss a ball to the child and begin a conversation about some of the unhelpful thoughts you've already talked about. Explain that you have been thinking about how you could both begin to "kick back" against these thoughts.

Suggest that you go first and ask the child to tell you an unhelpful thought that you could kick back for them. If the child feels uncertain about doing this you can tell the child that you had someone around their age recently who had some unhelpful thoughts. Use some examples, like "No one likes me" or "I'll never be able to do it" and work together with the child to find a way of kicking the thought back. For example, you could model some thoughts like "I have some good friends" and "I can try."

Ask the child to kick back some of your thoughts and encourage the child to come up with realistic or helpful thoughts as independently as possible.

FOR PARENTS

Parents may wish to be involved in a quick game at the end of the session if they have not participated during the session. Talk with parents about whether they could have a game of kick-back soccer at home and whether they could try to notice when their child kicks back against unhelpful thoughts.

DEVELOPMENTAL CONSIDERATIONS

Younger children often lack the ability to challenge their unhelpful thoughts and flexibly use helpful thinking in this way, so this activity is unlikely to be suitable for them. If you find, however, that a younger child is articulating a lot of unhelpful thoughts you may want use this activity to have them express these and encourage their parents to kick back with some helpful thoughts. Older children may also need support to think of suitable helpful thoughts, so having some they can choose from might help.

Lift the flap on anger

Children often respond quickly with anger in situations where they feel anxious, embarrassed or sad. This activity utilizes the concept of "lift the flap"—familiar to many children from picture books featuring flaps—to help them think about what feelings might underlie their anger.

MATERIALS

» You will need some cardboard, scissors, markers and pencils.

PROCEDURE

Explain to the child that you have been thinking a bit about them getting so angry and that you have been wondering whether there are any other feelings underneath this. Ask them if you could make a "lift the flap" together to explore this.

Depending on the child, you may first want to model an example of when you felt worried and got angry or similar. You can then ask about a recent example of a time when the child got angry and see if together you can discover whether there were any other feelings "hiding" beneath the anger.

Fold a cardboard sheet in half and cut three or four strips into the top piece so that when you open each you can see something underneath. Write or draw the feelings underneath as you work through some recent examples and write "anger" on the top of each flap, as shown in the *Lift the flap on anger example* opposite.

FOR PARENTS

Parents often find it easier to deal with feelings such as sadness or jealousy than anger. They may not be aware that this is how their child is feeling and may find themselves responding to the anger instead. Engaging them in this activity is particularly helpful as they will often see their child's behavior in a new way as a result.

If the child is struggling to identify any feelings other than anger, it may be helpful to encourage parents to start to gently explore this with their child in the moment as the emotions occur. Parents could acknowledge their child's anger, then wonder out loud whether their child is "sad angry," "hurt angry" or "jealous angry."

DEVELOPMENTAL CONSIDERATIONS

Younger children may be able to engage in this activity with the assistance of their parents. This would be particularly helpful in instances where you are encouraging the parents to think more about where their child is coming from and what they might be experiencing. If using this activity with younger children, try drawing faces rather than writing feelings words. Older children may find it easier to write feelings words and should be able to think of some examples of times when a different feeling was underneath their anger.

EXTENSION

It is also helpful to encourage parents to reflect on their own emotions and times when anger masks what else they might be feeling. You can ask that they try to identify this for themselves as well as their children. For example, they might be able to say "I'm worried we are going to be late so I'm starting to feel cross that you still don't have your shoes on."

Lift the flap on anger example

Mad Monday

Many children become anxious when things are not right or perfect, and can become very fixated on small details, often when the family is trying to get ready and leave in the morning. This activity provides families with a helpful and supportive way of challenging this, allowing the child to experience things not being quite right and realize that this is okay and can even be fun. This may challenge the child's anxious thoughts about things being not right, and may help them to try out and discover new ways to manage this. Completing this activity may also reveal other family members with similar challenges, which is important to know in order to work effectively with the family.

MATERIALS

» We tend to write a plan for this activity in the session for the family to take home; however, the activity itself does not require any additional materials.

PROCEDURE

Begin by explaining to the child that you know that they like to have things right and that they feel worried when things are not right. Explain that you have been wondering, however, what would happen if they woke up one morning and lots of things were not right. What if they woke up to find Dad with his dressing gown on backwards and his socks hanging from his ears? What if Mum was wearing her jumper inside out and their brother had his underwear on the outside of his trousers? This usually gets the family laughing and you can talk about what it would be like to have one mad day.

Ask the family about what they would do on a mad day. What would they wear? What would they eat? What would they do?

Once you have the ideas flowing, start to talk about what it would really be like to do this for a day:

• Who would find this the hardest?

• Who would find it the easiest?

• What would be hard about it?

• Is there anything that would make it easier?

Talk with the family about whether they could really do this and if so, when. Suggest a weekend day or a public holiday when the family will be at home.

When the family have settled on a day, suggest that they take some photos and send you them or bring some into the next session to show you. Reflect during the next session on what it was like to not have things right for the day. Find out who felt anxious and how long the anxiety lasted for. Work out what helped people to feel less anxious. Ask if they would do anything like that again and if so, what?

If the family don't undertake the activity, talk with them about why and reflect on how we sometimes want to avoid feelings of discomfort or anxiety. Reflect on how this is similar to what their child experiences and wonder about smaller goals, such as having an odd sock day.

FOR PARENTS

Parents should have had some introduction to understanding their child's anxiety prior to undertaking this activity. They should have some sense of the value of having their child sit with their anxiety and be comfortable with the idea of children facing their anxiety in small steps. Try to encourage open communication so that parents feel able to say if they don't feel comfortable with the idea. Praise them for their ability to be playful with their children and put themselves out of their own comfort zones.

DEVELOPMENTAL CONSIDERATIONS

Younger children are generally able to understand the concept of having a mixed-up day when supported to do so by their parents. They are often more focused on routine than older children; however, they should happily partake in this if their family is doing so. Even if they choose not to participate, seeing their family do so may be a useful experience and this can still be explored when they return to therapy.

Magic cord

This is a hands-on activity which uses the concrete prop of an elastic cord to symbolize the connection between children and their parents even when they are not together. It helps children to feel safer and still connected to their parents when they are separated, assisting with the common childhood difficulty of separation anxiety.

MATERIALS

» You will need a long piece of elastic ideally; however, either some string or some wool will work too.

» You will also need paper and markers.

PROCEDURE

Explain to the child that a long time ago they were in their mum's tummy. Ask a few questions about what they thought this might be like and explain that there was a special cord that was connected to their tummy so that they could have some of the food their mum was eating. Reflect on this and then explain that when babies are born there is another kind of magic cord—a special cord that connects children with their mums and dads (or other caregivers as relevant to the child). Draw the child as a baby and then ask them about what the cord should look like before you draw a cord connecting them to their mum and their dad. Explain that the cord is magical because it is very strong, can stretch an extremely long way and can never be broken. Say that you would like to make a pretend magic cord to play with. Use your wool, string or elastic to make a magic cord connecting the child to their mum and/or dad and then begin to experiment with it.

Talk about how far the string can stretch (over mountains and around the world) and how strong it is (not even a herd of elephants could break it). Demonstrate that the connection remains strong. Play with lots of examples before asking the parent or child if they think the magic cord stretches to childcare or preschool. Ask the parent about how they remember about the magic cord when they are at home or at work. Ask the child what they could do to remind them of the magic cord. Ask if they would like to take the string home as a way to show the rest of their family and tell them about the magic cord.

FOR PARENTS

It is important for parents to be involved in the play and discussions. For example, parents may join in experimenting with the magic cord, by walking outside the room holding one end of it and similar. It is common for parents to also experience anxiety about managing separations. This activity provides them with a helpful way to respond to their child's anxiety in the moment by reminding them of the magic cord.

DEVELOPMENTAL CONSIDERATIONS

Younger and older children tend to find this activity appealing. The activity makes the connection between children and parents apparent in a manner that is generally understandable for younger children. Younger children may need parents to remind them that the magic cord is just like the elastic as they may find it difficult to visualize this in the absence of having the elastic.

VARIATION

The idea of a string to represent social connections has been used elsewhere, for example in Patrice Karst and Geoff Stevenson's (2001) lovely picture book *The Invisible String*, which emphasizes a broader connectivity between everyone in the world.

EXTENSION

Parents can be encouraged to include the magic cord in their goodnight or goodbye rituals. For example, they could make up a silly routine saying "goodbye nose, goodbye hands, goodbye you, stretch magic cord and bring me back soon."

Magic spell

This activity provides a playful and imaginative way to teach children the concept of helpful thoughts and also to remind them to use helpful thoughts when they are anxious, angry or sad. The activity also helps parents to reflect on how their own responses can be helpful or unhelpful, and to consider modeling helpful thoughts.

MATERIALS

» You will need something to make a wand with. You can either purchase plain wood wands from craft stores or make one, using a popsicle stick, cardboard, and tape or glue.

» Paper and pens. You may also like to use glitter and glue to decorate the wand.

PROCEDURE

Explain to the child that you understand that their anger/worry/sadness has been very difficult for them and that you think that they could do with some magic to help. Suggest that you make a magic wand together and as you do so talk with the child and their parent about whether there are any magic words that help when they are feeling that way.

Some ideas for magic words to suggest include:

• I can have a go.

• I can do it.

• I'll be okay.

It can be helpful to make a big list of words that help. You can then ask the child to choose the magic words that they think are best and have them practice saying them with their wand. Try to aim for lots of swishing and drama.

Talk with the child and their parent about when they are most likely to need the wand. Who would be best to look after the wand? Who would be best to say the magic words? Is there anything they have to do while saying the words in order for them to be effective?

FOR PARENTS

Some parents will find this activity hard because they tend to respond to their child's emotions by trying to distract or redirect them and feel afraid to label them. Others will find it hard to know what to say. Uncovering these difficulties through this activity provides a great opportunity to work on these and can be identified as a goal for further work.

DEVELOPMENTAL CONSIDERATIONS

Younger children generally find it difficult to identify helpful or unhelpful thoughts. They often benefit from learning about the role helpful thoughts can play and having a helpful thought (or magic spell) that can assist them in a number of situations. Older children may also find this activity appealing and may enjoy showing you how they can use their wand in a range of situations, modifying the magic spell accordingly.

Mistake jars

Many children worry about making mistakes and often avoid tasks that are difficult for them as a result. This activity provides an experiential and concrete way of understanding the role of mistakes in learning and helps normalize mistakes, with the aim of reducing a child's anxiety about this.

MATERIALS

» You will need two large jars and some stickers or a marker to label these. You will also need something to fill them—you can choose counters, coins or stones, or if you prefer you can keep some paper and a pen by the jars.

PROCEDURE

Explain to the child that you are wondering about how they learn things. You may like to provide some developmentally appropriate examples, such as learning to read or learning to swim. If the child doesn't voluntarily talk about mistakes ask about these and whether they help or make learning harder.

Suggest that you do an experiment in which you label two jars, one for mistakes and one for learning (see the *Mistake jars example* opposite). Agree that everyone in the family will put a coin or counter in the appropriate jar when they make a mistake or learn something new. Alternatively, they could write down what they learnt or the mistake they made and put the paper in the appropriate jar.

Model how this is done by thinking of something you have learnt and a mistake you have made. Encourage the child to have a turn too. If the child's parents are in the session they can contribute at this time or may want to add to this later when you explain the experiment to them.

FOR PARENTS

Ensure that parents are aware of the aim of the experiment and know to watch for lots of learning so that the jars end up at least being even or the learning jar is fuller. Ask that the family bring the jars back to the next session so you can review what happened.

DEVELOPMENTAL CONSIDERATIONS

Younger children can be supported to benefit from this activity if their parents can help to draw out what the mistake they have made is and what the associated learning is, putting a token in each jar at the same time. Older children should be able to manage this more flexibly, having a greater awareness that the tokens in each jar will build over time and not necessarily needing each mistake or learning to be directly associated.

VARIATION

This activity can be easily adapted to working with a set of scales, weighing mistakes on one side and learning on the other. If you roll balls of play-doh or similar to represent the mistakes and learning, you can increase the complexity and talk about big versus little mistakes and different kinds of learning. This is often helpful for older children who are more able to understand that when learning something that is very new or very complex, you are likely to make a larger number of mistakes.

Mistake jars example

Monster hunt

Young children are often fearful of monsters and the dark. However, they are at an age where they often find it hard to articulate their thoughts in relation to this and find it difficult to benefit from working abstractly around this. This activity provides a concrete way to help children face their fear of monsters in a supportive and playful context and to challenge some of their unhelpful thoughts.

MATERIALS

» You may like to use some dress-ups, or could make some masks or create some tools, such as a "monster sucker-upperer."

PROCEDURE

Ask the child lots of questions about the monsters in a way that gently challenges them. Try to express your curiosity and a desire to learn more about the monsters.

Here are some to try:

- Where are the monsters?

- Are they there all the time? If not, where do they go?

- What do they eat? How do they get food?

- What do they look like? How come you've never seen them?

- Don't they get bored hiding all day? Wouldn't they like to come out and play with your toys?

It is helpful to involve parents at this stage. For example, you could ask their mum, "Have you ever noticed any food missing from the kitchen? Do you ever notice monster prints when you do the vacuuming?"

Agree that if there are monsters it is going to be important to find them and suggest that the family go on a monster hunt. You can then ask a number of questions to prepare them for the hunt. Here are some example questions:

- Who will we need to go on the hunt?

- What would we need to take?

- Do we need any special gear?

- Where will we need to look?

It's helpful to make something with the family that they can then take on the hunt as this is a way of linking the session with what will happen at home. Here are some suggestions about what you could make:

- super monster spotting goggles

- monster buster hats for everyone who will go on the hunt

- a monster sucker-upperer.

Plan with the family when they will do the hunt and reflect on how the hunt went during the next session.

FOR PARENTS

It is important to explain your aim to parents so that they feel confident in completing this exercise. Some will be more open to this sort of play than others so acknowledging that this may feel silly is important. Emphasizing the importance of children learning through play rather than talking is helpful and often you can identify one parent who will be more comfortable leading this. Often this activity is very helpful even if the family do not do the monster hunt at home.

DEVELOPMENTAL CONSIDERATIONS

Younger children often have a terrific imagination, which allows them to enjoy and engage well with this activity. Making hands-on props for younger children is particularly useful as it means the family will be more likely to try using these at home, which helps younger children to challenge some of their ideas about monsters. Older children will be more able to engage in discussion around monsters, which will serve to challenge some of their unhelpful thoughts.

Possibilities jump

Learning to problem solve is an important part of therapy with children and is commonly used by therapists working within a CBT framework. This activity introduces problem solving to children in a concrete manner, allowing them to have a hands-on experience of problem solving and, more specifically, of generating and evaluating a range of behavioral options. It also encourages children to try out and discover new behavioral responses.

MATERIALS

» You will need something to jump on to. This could be some cushions, some discs or even some sheets of paper. If using paper you may like to write the options the child comes up with on the paper.

PROCEDURE

When talking with the child about possible ways of managing a problem, suggest that you try these options out. Have the child generate some options and allocate a cushion, disc or sheet of paper for each option, dropping these around the floor.

Suggest to the child that you try the options out and ask them to choose which they would like to try first. When the child has chosen an option, ask them to stand or sit on that option and help them to reflect on how they would feel about that option, what they think about it and what would be likely to happen.

Encourage the child to complete this process with all of the options. Then ask what they think about each of the options and which they would like to try. Are there any options they would not try?

FOR PARENTS

This is a good one to demonstrate for parents if they have not been in the room for the activity. It is worth explaining to them that this is like the process of brainstorming we often use as adults and suggesting that this is something they could try at home. It is helpful to encourage parents to allow children to try any of the options they come up with, provided of course they are not dangerous, and evaluate them. Allowing children to try out solutions and evaluate whether or not they were helpful is a good way of building resilience.

DEVELOPMENTAL CONSIDERATIONS

Younger children are likely to find it difficult to imagine how they will feel in a given situation, making it difficult for them to evaluate each of the possibilities. Helping younger children to list some possibilities, however, is often helpful and this activity provides a helpful visual way of reinforcing that they do have some choices. Younger children can be encouraged to choose something different to try and asked to let you know how this choice goes next time they attend therapy.

Pushing my buttons

This activity uses the common saying "pushing my buttons" to help children to identify and express triggers to a range of emotions, including worry, anger, sadness and happiness. Incorporating a hands-on, active element makes it a very useful and enjoyable activity.

MATERIALS

» You will need a set of colored discs. You will need about four different colors, with three to four discs of each.

» You will need a set of colored discs to represent large buttons. You will need about four different colors, with three to four buttons in each color. You may like to photocopy the *Pushing my buttons template* on page 163 onto different color sheets of cardboard or, if you have them available, use beanbags or cushions as the buttons.

PROCEDURE

Begin by asking the child if they have ever heard the saying "It's pushing my buttons." Explain that it is about having something that particularly upsets you. Say that you would like to know about all the things that make the child feel happy as well as those that make them sad, angry and worried.

Suggest that you use some "buttons" to help you think about this. Have the child choose a color for each emotion. Explain that you will pop these on the floor each time they tell you about something that makes them feel that way. Proceed in this way until you have worked through all of the emotions.

Once you have done this you can have the child hop over all the happy ones prior to packing them up.

FOR PARENTS

Parents may be particularly helpful in assisting younger children to think about their triggers and this activity can be adapted so that you all take a turn to talk about what makes you feel a particular emotion. This is often preferable for younger children who may be less able to articulate their emotions and triggers.

You may also talk with parents about what pushes their buttons, as reflecting on this is often helpful when you are supporting parents to best help their children.

DEVELOPMENTAL CONSIDERATIONS

Younger children find this activity appealing, though they may find it difficult to think of what causes them to feel various feelings. Being able to model examples and provide suggestions often helps. Having parents participate can also help with this and the activity is often a useful way of extending the family's awareness about the child's feelings. Older children are also likely to enjoy this activity and it may be particularly appealing to those who prefer activities that enable them to be out of their seats.

VARIATIONS

If you use colored buttons for this, children can thread these and wear them home as a reminder of what you have talked about.

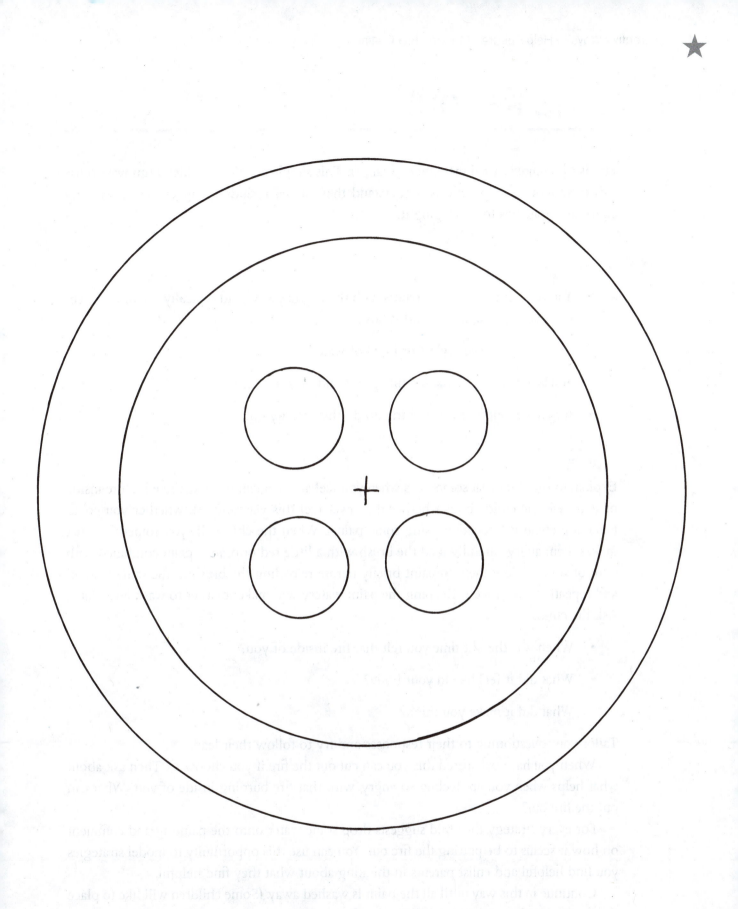

Pushing my buttons template

Put the fire out

Fire is a commonly used metaphor for anger. This simple activity provides a fun way to use this metaphor to help children understand their anger, including triggers, early warning signs and strategies for managing it.

MATERIALS

» You will need watercolor paints with the colors you would typically use to represent fire, such as orange, red and yellow.

» You will also need a glass or bowl of water.

» You will need some plain white paper and maybe scissors.

» It may be helpful to have a tray to do this activity on.

PROCEDURE

Explain to the child that sometimes when you feel angry it can feel like there is a fire inside of you. Ask the child about whether they ever feel this way and ask whether you could make a pretend fire together using some paints. When the child tells you something that makes them angry carefully load the brush with a little red or orange paint combined with a lot of water. Allow them to paint briefly before reloading the brush in the same manner and repeating the process. Keeping the paint watery will make it easier to wash away later. Ask the child:

• When was the last time you felt that fire inside of you?

• What did it feel like in your body?

• What did it make you think?

Tailor your questioning to their responses and try to follow their lead.

When you have exhausted this you can cut out the fire if you choose to. Then ask about what helps when you are feeling so angry, with that fire burning inside of you. What can put the fire out?

For every strategy the child suggests drop some water onto the painting and comment on how it seems to be putting the fire out. You can use this opportunity to model strategies you find helpful and enlist parents in thinking about what they find helpful.

Continue in this way until all the paint is washed away. (Some children will like to place the fire in the glass or bowl, which is also fine and should wash the paint away.)

FOR PARENTS

Try to involve parents in this activity, asking about what makes them feel that angry fire inside and what they find helps.

Talk about early warning signs and agree that parents will try to let their child know that they seem to be getting angry so they can make a good choice. For some children this will be easiest if a parent quietly speaks to them, while for others something fun (like pretending to be a smoke alarm and beeping) will work well.

DEVELOPMENTAL CONSIDERATIONS

This activity is appealing to both younger and older children. The metaphor is a simple one that most younger children will readily understand. Using simpler language when discussing this activity with younger children is important, while completing this activity with older children provides lots of opportunity to develop their emotional vocabulary and awareness of how they experience anger.

EXTENSION

Talk with the child about what they will do if they feel the fire building inside of them. Explain that you have someone of around the same age who is coming to see you that often gets a big angry fire inside of them and ends up shouting at others and hurting them. Ask the child if they have any advice for this child. You may want to write them a quick letter together.

Rocket chair

Sometimes children are unable to envisage how things could be different, which prevents them from trying anything new and contributes to feelings of hopelessness. This playful and imaginative activity helps children to better understand their experience, such as their current emotional difficulties, and to see and even try out other possibilities by visiting other worlds.

MATERIALS

» You will need two chairs, some free space in the clinic room and a good imagination.

PROCEDURE

Explain to the child that you are a bit tired of the clinic room and would like to go somewhere different. Say that you have a couple of rocket chairs and ask the child if they would like to come flying with you.

Sit in the rocket chairs and make some funny lifting-off sounds. Ask the child what planet or land they would like to go to. Land wherever they suggest and have fun pretending to explore the place.

When you return to the rocket ship suggest somewhere that is clinically relevant to the child. This could be Grouchland, Happytown or the Worryzone. As before, pretend to land and explore the place. You can think about what tools might help you on the planet, what the landscape might be like, etc.

When you are back in the rockets you can reflect on what that place felt like, what they most liked/disliked and whether they would like to visit again.

FOR PARENTS

You can explain the parallels between a child's life and what they have played out for parents and help parents to understand what you thought they learnt from the experience.

DEVELOPMENTAL CONSIDERATIONS

Some younger children will happily engage in this activity, though it will be important to keep your language simpler and you will, most likely, need to provide more structure. For example, you might visit Happytown and Grouchland and keep your reflections centered on how each felt. Older children will generally be more able to engage in this task, though some may be reluctant to engage in imaginative play. Children with ASD are likely to find the creative demands of the task and the less structured nature challenging and it may be best avoided for these children.

Scary sounds game

The dark is often a source of anxiety for children and they can become very anxious in response to the noises that they hear at night. This game provides a hands-on way of helping them to think about what else might be making the noises.

MATERIALS

> » You will need a range of sound-making materials—such as spoons, sticks, bits of fabric, a cup, a plate, a hard piece of plastic, different kitchen utensils and the like. You will also need a blindfold.

PROCEDURE

Explain to the child and parent that you have been thinking about some of the sounds that scare them at night time and wondered about what sort of scary sounds you could make together.

Explain that you will use a blindfold and take it in turns to guess what the other person used to make the sound. Challenge the child by saying that you want them to make the scariest sound they can.

While you are playing, ask about whether there is anything in their house that makes a sound like that. Talk about what else it could be at home that makes that noise—is it a tree branch against the window or is there a squeaky floorboard? Parents can be particularly helpful in this regard and you can often engage them and the child in a conversation around the sounds that their house makes, explaining that all houses make sounds at times.

FOR PARENTS

Parents are often very quick to reassure their children and can be unintentionally dismissive of their fears. Parents can be encouraged to reflect that the noise sounds scary and ask children what they think could have made the noise, rather than providing reassurance too quickly.

DEVELOPMENTAL CONSIDERATIONS

This hands-on activity will appeal to both younger and older children. Younger children are likely to find it harder to generalize from the examples presented in session to the sounds they hear at home. Involving parents in this activity will enable them to support children with this at home too.

VARIATIONS

Scary shadows is also a fun game to play, using a torch and an assortment of objects and cardboard to cut out.

EXTENSION

Night Noises written by Mem Fox and illustrated by Terry Denton is a popular children's story that can be fun to read and reflect on following this activity (Fox and Denton 2005).

Strain it out

This activity provides a concrete way for children to consider the role their thoughts have on their emotions and behavior. We use this activity to help children consider which thoughts are helpful to focus on and hold onto, and which thoughts are better to let go of. It can also be used to introduce the concept of the transient nature of thoughts, and can help children to develop a more balanced point of view of their situation.

MATERIALS

> » For younger children it is helpful to have a strainer and some uncooked pasta (lasagne sheets or penne) and a marker. For older children it may be sufficient simply to draw a strainer, like the *Strain it out example* overleaf.

PROCEDURE

Begin by asking the child if they have ever watched their parents cook pasta. Ask about what they do when the pasta is cooked. Talk about why straining the pasta is important and ask questions about whether they would want to eat the pasta with the water left in.

Talk with the child about how in some ways our minds are like strainers. Lots of different thoughts come into our brain. Some are helpful and some are not. Thoughts come into our brain and usually just drain away again like the cooking water, without us having to do anything to let them go. This is happening all the time as thoughts come and go. However, sometimes we can get a thought stuck in our mind, or we can choose to keep a thought in mind.

Begin talking with the child about some of the things that come into their mind and what happens when those things are in their mind. Ask about what they do and how they feel. Children can be asked whether this is something they would like to let drain away (like the cooking water) or something they would like to keep in mind. For younger children, you can label the uncooked pasta with a marker to represent those thoughts that they would like to keep in mind. For older children you can label the thoughts they would like to keep as you draw pasta in the strainer and make lines to represent those things they would prefer to strain away (much in the way that cooking water does).

FOR PARENTS

It may be helpful to have parents present for this activity, particularly if you have a child who is very depressed and is unlikely to generate helpful thoughts and positive memories.

Explaining the activity to parents and encouraging them to watch for moments when their children let the unhelpful bits strain away is helpful. Parents can be asked to think about what helps the child to manage this better as well as notice those times when this is harder.

DEVELOPMENTAL CONSIDERATIONS

Younger and older children can both benefit from this activity, though it may be too complex and abstract for some young children to understand. If using this with younger children, it is important to involve their parents in the activity, to assist in generating relevant examples and to enhance the parent's own understanding of these concepts. In this way, it can be used with younger children to identify helpful thoughts or self-talk that they can use and their parents can prompt.

EXTENSION

If you use penne or similar, you can thread the labeled pieces onto a lace or piece of wool to create a necklace or garland of helpful thoughts and positive memories.

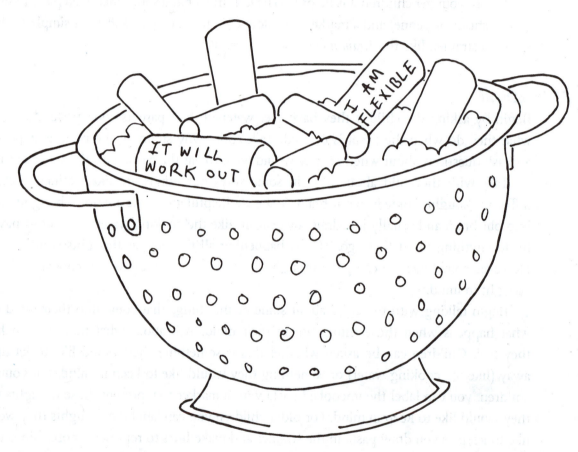

Strain it out example

Straw that broke the camel's back

This simple game with blocks was developed to help children understand how anger can build up if not expressed, and then later explode, sometimes in response to something relatively small. Building the child's awareness and understanding of their own tendency to do this may help them to notice when it happens, allowing them to consider alternatives to holding in their anger, and reducing their confusion when they do feel upset about something trivial. The hands-on game provides visual cues to support the child's learning.

MATERIALS

» You will need some wooden blocks that can be stacked one on top of the other.

PROCEDURE

Explain that you have noticed that sometimes children hold in their anger about lots of things until it finally gets too much and then they explode. Suggest that you play a game with the blocks to help you think about this. Take it in turns to place a block down saying something that makes you angry. Try to use a feeling word that describes the level of anger when you place a block down. Use words like annoyed, frustrated, furious or mad depending on what you are describing. Take it in turns to build the tower higher and higher.

When the tower falls, reflect on how this is a bit like an explosion of anger. Try to engage the child in some conversation about what it is like when they explode. Talk about what finally made the tower fall. Was it something big or something little? If it was something little you can talk about the saying "the straw that broke the camel's back."

FOR PARENTS

This is a really helpful activity for explaining to parents why children may be so quick to anger when returning home from school. Often they have contained their anger about a lot of things at school and when something happens at home it can be the final straw. This may lead to a helpful discussion about what parents can do to provide the child with some time and space to recover to avoid this situation.

DEVELOPMENTAL CONSIDERATIONS

Younger children may find this concept too difficult to understand, though those with good language skills may be able to. Older children generally understand the metaphor when it is presented with examples.

EXTENSION

Children may like to draw the straws that build up on their back, labeling them as they draw.

Target practice

Increasing a child's language around feelings and helping them to understand that feelings range in intensity is often a focus of therapy. This scaling activity provides a hands-on way of assisting children to recognize and label lower levels of anxiety or anger, and to consider using calming strategies before their feelings escalate.

MATERIALS

» You will need a soft ball for this, one that is safe to throw around the clinic room. To make the target you can use either some butcher's paper, stuck to the wall with blu-tack (poster putty), or draw a target on a large whiteboard if you have one in the room.

PROCEDURE

Begin by asking the child if they would like to play a throwing game and suggesting that you draw up a target. Suggest that you put a feeling word in the middle and use the outer circles to list lower levels of this feeling. Choose a feeling for the middle that is relevant for the child, such as worry, fear or anger. Together with the child come up with some words that mean a little worried or a little angry. Talk and decide together about where these words might go on the target. See the *Target practice example* presented opposite.

Once the target is set up you can take turns throwing the ball at it and describing a time when you have experienced that feeling. We also like to talk with children about what they did in that situation, or what they think a helpful response would be, to reinforce coping strategies.

FOR PARENTS

Parents can readily be included in this game. If they have not been in the room it is easy to have the child explain the game to them and allow them to have a quick turn when they join you. It is helpful to provide them with a rationale about extending the child's emotional vocabulary and helping them to recognize lower levels of anger or anxiety if you have not already done so. If you have used paper stuck up on the wall it is easy to give this to the child so that they can play the target game at home. If not, you could suggest that they notice times when they experience the feelings listed on the target until the next session.

DEVELOPMENTAL CONSIDERATIONS

Both older and younger children will enjoy this activity. Younger children will need more support to think about other words for feelings and it is often helpful to include parents so that you can draw on words that are commonly used within the family home.

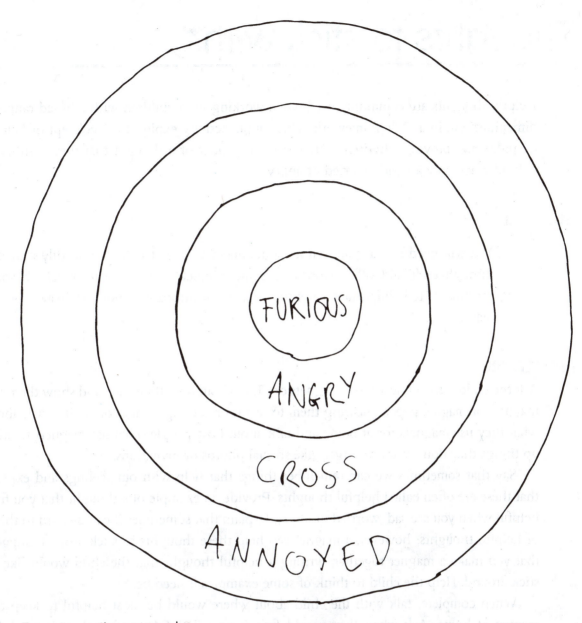

Target practice example

Thoughts to stick with

Helpful thoughts are commonly used when working with children with a broad range of difficulties within a CBT framework. This simple activity explores the concept of helpful thoughts and provides children with a visual reminder of a thought that they identify as helpful when they are sad, worried or angry.

MATERIALS

» You will need markers and either some magnetic paper (which is readily available through craft and office stores) or some magnets that you can attach to some cardboard. It is important to ensure that the cardboard is not too heavy for the magnets.

PROCEDURE

Ask the child if they know what magnets do. Talk about how they stick and show them the magnets or magnet paper, allowing them to test it on a filing cabinet or similar. Ask about what they use magnets for at home and talk about how people often use magnets to stick up things they don't want to forget, like special photos or invitations.

Say that sometimes we can remember things that help with our feelings and explain that these are often called helpful thoughts. Provide an example of a thought that you find helpful when you are sad, worried or angry. Explain that sometimes it can be hard to think of helpful thoughts; however, a magnet can help these thoughts to stick around. Suggest that you make a magnet together, writing a helpful thought that the child would like to stick around. Help the child to think of some examples if need be.

When complete, talk with the child about where would be most helpful to keep the magnet at home. Ask when they would find it most helpful to remember that helpful thought. Talk with the child about whether there is anyone who could remind them of this thought and ask what would be the best way they could be reminded.

FOR PARENTS

If parents are in the session, they may like to create a magnet of something that they find it helpful to remember. For example, they may like to make a magnet saying "It's okay for my house to be messy" or "I am doing my best."

Have the child show their parent their magnet if they were not in the session for this activity. Talk about how this is a helpful visual reminder and explore with the parent how they could remind their child to look at this.

DEVELOPMENTAL CONSIDERATIONS

Both older and younger children will enjoy this activity. You will need to choose thoughts that suit the child's developmental level, with simpler thoughts that generalize across situations being more appropriate for younger children. Younger children will also be limited by their reading ability with this activity so you may like to draw a picture that represents the thought.

Toilet paper scaling

This is a scaling activity to assist with anger management. It was developed to help children begin to think about different levels of anger and how these feel different and require different responses. The use of toilet paper can be amusing and fun for children, helping them to relax and engage. This activity could be easily varied to address anxiety.

MATERIALS

» You will need a roll of toilet paper, some markers and scissors.

PROCEDURE

Explain to the child that sometimes you can be a little bit angry and sometimes you can be very angry and that there are other steps in between too. Explain that you are going to use the toilet paper to play a game with this.

Ask the child how many squares would be good for a little bit angry and tear these off. Try to think of a couple of other words for this, like annoyed, and jot them down on the paper. Talk about how this feels in the child's body, anything they tend to think and the like and make a note of these on the paper too. See the *Toilet paper scaling example* provided opposite.

Then ask the child about feeling a little more angry:

• How many more squares would you need?

• What are some words for feeling that angry? (Maybe cross?)

• How does that feel in your body?

• When did you last feel that way?

• What were you thinking?

Continue in this way until you have as many levels as the child wants and you have included the most angry level—probably "rage" or "fury."

When this is done, explain that it can be hard to not get caught up in anger and show the child what you mean by wrapping each of the pieces around them. If the child is reluctant to do this you can let them wrap you up and reflect on how this feels.

Take the scissors and express that cutting through anger can be difficult, particularly the rage or fury which is so long, big and strong. Say that all feelings are okay and so is anger; however, it is important to make sure that you don't hurt anyone or break anything when you are angry. Explain that sometimes being able to calm down is important and ask if they have any ideas for cutting through the anger. Make a cut for each idea, reflecting on each and asking about whether the child has used that idea while cutting. Continue this until the toilet paper is all cut away and the child is free, congratulating them on doing such a good job.

FOR PARENTS

If parents are not in the room, you might want to show them the remnants and let the child tell them what they learnt. Parents may be happy to reinforce these ideas at home by asking how many squares of anger their child is feeling when appropriate.

DEVELOPMENTAL CONSIDERATIONS

This activity is well suited to older children as younger children may find it too abstract. If you do want to modify it for use with younger children, you could do so by having them show you how angry they felt with their hands and measuring the toilet paper so that it fits that space. Drawing pictures as well as writing feelings words would also make the activity more accessible to younger children.

Toilet paper scaling example

Treasure chest

Most therapists who work with children within a CBT framework will encourage helpful thoughts, or positive self-talk, as a way in which children can manage their emotions. This activity provides a way to teach children some helpful thoughts and to encourage them to use these when they are worried, angry or upset.

MATERIALS

» You will need a box—you can buy pre-cut treasure chests that you can fold up yourself or you may prefer to decorate a tissue box or similar.

» You will also need cardboard, scissors and markers or pencils to make cards to go in the box.

PROCEDURE

Once you have developed some behavioral strategies that the child is using to manage their anxiety or anger, you can talk about whether there is anything that they find helpful to remember when they feel angry, worried or sad.

You may need to suggest some helpful thoughts and record these on the cardboard for the child, cutting them up and putting them in the treasure chest. Try to draw a picture that represents the helpful thought for the child if they are young.

Some ideas for helpful thoughts include:

- I can do this.

- I can ask for help.

- It will be okay.

- I can try.

- I can calm down.

Keep these simple for the child and try to choose thoughts that will relate to multiple situations.

Talk with the child about when their treasure chest might be useful and where they might keep it.

Some children may be able to engage in a conversation about how their brain is like a treasure chest and how it can provide lots of helpful thoughts that can help keep them calm.

FOR PARENTS

Parents can easily be included in the creation of the treasure chest and will often be able to come up with some helpful thoughts. They can be encouraged to help children recall some of the helpful thoughts when they see them becoming anxious, angry or upset.

DEVELOPMENTAL CONSIDERATIONS

Younger children are still developing an awareness of their thoughts; however, they often benefit from learning about helpful thoughts and having some that they can use across a range of situations. They find it difficult to identify helpful thoughts and will generally need the therapist to assist with this. Older children should be more able to generate some helpful thoughts of their own, though many will need support to do so.

VARIATIONS

It may also be helpful to include cards with reminders about behavioral strategies that the child has been using to manage strong feelings. This may include a picture of bubble breathing, active strategies (e.g. star jumps or jumping on the trampoline) or a relaxation CD.

EXTENSION

Try engaging in some role play and act out some situations that the child finds anxiety-provoking, asking if they can help you with their treasure chest. Model that you feel better when you remember these things.

Similarly, you can have the child use puppets or role play to act out a situation that would typically cause them to be angry. Get them to show you with their hands how angry they are to start with and then how angry they are after they remember each of things in the treasure chest.

Warning signs

Children and parents both benefit from a greater awareness of early warning signs for an emotional difficulty the child has been experiencing. This not only builds their awareness of their emotions, but also provides the opportunity to intervene sooner before feelings escalate. This craft activity provides children and families with a fun way to explore this concept, and a visual reminder to take home to assist with generalization.

MATERIALS

» You will need some popsicle sticks, cardboard, glue and markers to make the signs and some play-doh or clay to stick them in.

PROCEDURE

Explain that you think the child is very good at noticing, which is a great skill to have. Ask how they came to see you today and what they noticed on the way. Ask whether they noticed any signs and if so what they were. Talk about the different kinds of signs that can be seen and the functions of these. Talk about warning signs and the important role they have. Explain that you are curious to know what the child has noticed about their own early warning signs. For example, do they start to feel hot and does their voice get louder when they are angry? Or does their heart beat faster and their jaw tighten when they feel worried? Suggest that together you make some early warning signs, such as shown in the *Warnings signs example* opposite.

Working together, begin making some early warning signs that indicate that the child is beginning to experience whichever emotion you are working on. Draw the sign on yellow cardboard or use white cardboard and color it yellow. Use a picture or words to depict what the early warning sign is and glue these to the popsicle stick when completed.

When you have a number of warning signs ready you can use your play-doh or clay to make stands for them and have the child position them as though on a road, indicating which is the first thing they notice right through to those signs that mean danger is imminent. Alternatively, if you have a lot of clay you can fashion a road and have the child stick them directly in to that.

FOR PARENTS

This is a valuable activity for parents as it increases their awareness of their child's early warning signs and enables them to provide support at those times. Involving parents in a discussion about early warning signs and having them notice their own early warning signs is particularly helpful. Doing so normalizes the experience for children, reminding them that even adults can have emotions that get too big at times. Further, parents who experience difficulty regulating their own emotions may find this helpful.

DEVELOPMENTAL CONSIDERATIONS

Younger children will need assistance to understand the concept of early warning signs; however, they may be able to complete this activity with the assistance of their parent and the therapist. Often identifying early warning signs is of particular value to parents, so having parents involved is valuable for both younger and older children.

Warning signs example

What lives in your house?

This craft activity involves constructing the child's house, which functions as a metaphor for family, and using this to explore emotions within the family and to review progress. It provides a non-confrontational and hands-on way to review what the child's current experience is, celebrate achievements, identify emotions that continue to be troubling and build the family's motivation to work on these.

MATERIALS

> » You will need a box or cardboard to construct a house, along with markers, pencils, scissors and glue.

> » It is helpful to have additional cardboard or paper that can be pasted onto or placed in the house.

PROCEDURE

Introduce the activity by saying that you want to get a sense of what things are like at home now. You have been wondering whether things have changed and would like to hear the child's ideas about this. Suggest that you make a house together to help you think about this.

Create a basic house from the box or cardboard, adding in any details the child wants, which may include physical features, like doors and windows, or the family members who live there.

Ask about any feelings that live in the house. Help the child to draw these or write them on a strip of cardboard so that they can be added to the house. Talk with the child about where these belong—have they left the house now, are they part way out the door or do they stay close to one person in particular?

Ask about whether the child would like this to be different:

- In what way would they like it to be different?

- Would the house change as a result?

- What would it be like?

- How could the feeling be shifted out of the door or thrown out of a window?

FOR PARENTS

This activity can be done either with the whole family, with a subset of the family or with the child alone. Parents and children may work on the activity together, or they may complete separate houses, with an opportunity for comparison afterwards. Parents can be asked where they could keep the model within the house and what they will remember when they see it.

DEVELOPMENTAL CONSIDERATIONS

Younger children may need some support to enable them to think about the feelings that reside in their home, as home in this activity functions as a metaphor for family. Having parents and other siblings in the room is helpful when you are working with younger children as they will provide examples that support the child to think about this.

EXTENSION

This activity can be extended into helpful discussions around what anger or worry does to the child. How does it make them act/look/feel? What would they like to do or say to the anger or the worry?

Which animal?

Children struggle with more formal problem solving; however, play provides a natural way of exploring and evaluating different possibilities for responses and behaviors. This activity uses play with the familiar medium of toy animals to help children try out and practice new responses to situations they find challenging.

MATERIALS

» You will need a set of toy animals for this activity. It is important that the set includes a good range of animals. For example, there should be some smaller animals and some larger ones (e.g. an insect, bird, lion and giraffe) and some should be fierce, while others should be meek (e.g. a butterfly as opposed to a tiger).

PROCEDURE

Begin by suggesting to the child that you might play with some animals. Look briefly at the animals, talking about how they are quite different. Introduce a scenario that is relevant to the child, such as not wanting to go to zoo school, and ask that they choose three or four different animals to deal with this problem. Remind the child that all of the animals will have a different way of managing this. Role-playing with each animal in turn, ask that the child show you how each animal might respond.

Questions that you might like to ask include:

• What will they do if…?

• How do they feel when…?

• Is there something that helps them to…?

When the child has shown you how the various animals managed the situation, talk with them about which animal they thought managed best and why. Ask what advice that animal might have for the others.

If the child feels comfortable with this, you can ask further questions about how this relates to their experience. This might include:

• Which animal are you most like?

• Which animal would you most like to be like?

• How would things be different if you were more like that animal?

• How could you remember to be more like that animal?

• What would help you to be more like that animal?

FOR PARENTS

Parents can readily be included in this activity, participating by enacting some of the animals. If they are not present, you can have the child show the animal they would most like to be or the one that they thought had the most helpful advice. Talk with them about how they can help their child to be more like this animal and what might help their child to remember to use this strategy.

DEVELOPMENTAL CONSIDERATIONS

Older children will readily understand this activity and should be able to generate different responses for the animals. Younger children will need more help and you will need to model how various animals will respond.

EXTENSION

If you feel comfortable doing so, you may like to let the child take the animal home as a reminder, looking after it until the next session. Otherwise you might like to make a drawing or poster to remind the child of what they discovered. Taking a photo on their parent's phone or tablet is another good way of encouraging generalization of these skills to other settings.

Worry box

A worry box is a simple and frequently used activity aimed at providing a non-threatening way of helping children to verbalize their worries and then to put them aside or away rather than continue to focus on them. This can be containing for anxious children. We describe here our approach to the worry box, which we complete as a hands-on activity with children coupled with therapeutic conversations that incorporate elements of scaling and of the narrative technique of externalizing the problem.

MATERIALS

» You can use a box of any description. Plain matchboxes are readily available for purchase and are often particularly attractive for children.

» You will need markers or pencils along with some paper and scissors.

PROCEDURE

Explain to the child that everyone worries sometimes and that you have been wondering about what worries them. Tell them that you thought it would be helpful to make a special box to put their worries in.

Encourage the child to decorate their box, while talking with them about what they think the box should look like. You can also ask about whether there are lots of worries to put in the box or just a few, whether they are big or little worries and the like.

You may like to make a box of your own so that you can model being able to talk about some of your worries. Similarly if a parent is involved in the session they may like to make one.

When the child is finished decorating the box you can take it in turns to write down or draw some worries and pop them in the box.

Talk with the child when you are done about what they might like to do with the box. You might ask:

• Where will they keep it when they get home?

• How does the box feel?

• Where were the worries before they were in the box?

• What were the worries doing before they were in the box?

• How will things be different now that they are in the box?

• What will they do if they have some more worries when they get home?

• Did writing them down help?

FOR PARENTS

Explain to parents that being able to express what you are worried about is a very important first step. Encourage them to try to gently interpret what a child may be worried about and to remind the child about their worry box if they need reminding.

DEVELOPMENTAL CONSIDERATIONS

Worry boxes are suitable for both younger and older children. If using the activity with younger children, provide a larger box, and ask them to draw the worries. They may like you to write the name of the worry next to their drawing. They are likely to need more support from their parents at home to continue to express their worries and use their worry box. Older children may prefer to keep their worry box private. They often prefer smaller worry boxes, such as a matchbox size.

VARIATIONS

Some children prefer to use a journal or a sketchbook to record their feelings. Still others might prefer to do a video diary about how their day has been. Worry dolls can also be a way in which some children can reflect regularly on their feelings and others are able to tell the family pet.

Variations on the worry box can be found online and in other books. For example, Huebner (2005) describes locking worries in an imaginary worry box. In their self-help book, Romain and Verdick (2000) suggest that children use a worry jar to write down their worries and trap them in the jar, and Stallard (2002) similarly suggests children make their own worry safe.

EXTENSION

If you have access to the book, *The Huge Bag of Worries* by Virginia Ironside and illustrated by Frank Rodgers (2004), you might like to read this book together with the child. This may be useful to gently encourage the child to share the worries from their worry box with someone, if and when this is relevant for the particular child (so perhaps at a later session). The main character in the book takes the worries from her bag and sorts through them with an old lady, who shows her that some disappear once shared, others belong to other people, etc., which may be beneficial for some children to consider in relation to their own worries.

Yawn game

In families, when one member feels sad, angry or worried, other members can "catch" that feeling, which can result in unhelpful responses and further escalation of emotions. This is a brief game to play with families or subsets of families to help family members realize that feelings can be contagious and identify how this occurs within their own family.

MATERIALS

We tend to plan ahead for this activity; however, no materials are required.

PROCEDURE

Begin by giving an exaggerated yawn and watching what happens. Point out if anyone yawned in response to your yawn and anyone who yawned in response to their yawn.

Talk about how yawning can be catchy and ask the family whether they have noticed other feelings that sometimes catch in their family. Ask questions about who is most prone to catching the feelings of others, whether there is anyone who can stop the pattern and the like.

Talk about how positive feelings can be catchy too and ask about whether anyone thinks they could set up a contagious laugh or smile. Ask them to do so in the session and reflect on what happens.

FOR PARENTS

Parents often respond to their child's feelings in kind. Highlighting this tendency and helping them to find alternative ways to respond can be particularly helpful in supporting them to better support their children.

DEVELOPMENTAL CONSIDERATIONS

Both younger and older children will enjoy playing this game and should be able to understand at a simple level that people can catch the feelings of others. Younger children will find it hard to think about how this relates to their experiences within the family, though some older children may be able to do so. It is parents who we ask to take responsibility for this, though, and it is with parents that we focus our discussion around how this occurs at home and what can be done to alter this.

EXTENSION

Ask about any times lately when family members have caught a feeling or nominate someone to be on "contagious feeling watch." You could give a child a whistle to blow or similar when they notice feelings becoming catching. Even if children don't follow through with this at home, often an activity like this heightens the family's awareness and can lead to some behavioral changes.

Some parents will be interested to know, and more likely to take on these ideas, if you share with them that the contageous nature of feelings seems to be supported by neuro-scientific evidence relating to mirror neurons (brain cells which fire when we observe other people's emotions, influencing our own emotions). Siegel and Bryson (2012) provide a simple explanation of this.

Appendix: Our Favorite Children's Books for Therapy

Baa! Moo! What Will We Do? by A.H. Benjamin and Jane Chapman and publisher Little Tiger Press Group—explores how worrying about new events can be unhelpful.

Go Away, Mr Worrythoughts! and *Happythoughts are Everywhere…* by Nicky Johnston and published by Nicky's Art—incorporates externalization, visualization, positive thinking and practical strategies in two stories about a boy who overcomes his anxiety.

Is a Worry Worrying You? written by Ferida Wolff and Harriet May Savitz, with illustrations by Marie Letourneau and published by Tanglewood Press—approaches worries with the use of humour, externalization and creative problem solving.

Liking Myself written by Pat Palmer, illustrated by Sue Rama and published by Boulden Pub—a longer book with activities to complete inside, useful for encouraging older children to listen to and talk about all different feelings.

Mr Huff by Anna Walker and published by Penguin Books—explores bad days, unhappy feelings, acceptance of emotions, and hope.

Some Bunny to Talk to: A Story About Going to Therapy by Cheryl Sterling, Paola Conte and Larissa Labay, illustrated by Tiphanie Beeke and published by American Psychological Association—a book that introduces young children to therapy, helping them to understand what to expect.

The Frightened Little Owl written by Mark Ezra, illustrated by Gavin Rowe and published by Little Tiger Press Group—a story for younger children about overcoming fears and finding the courage to try things on your own.

The Grouchies written by Debbie Wagenbach, illustrated by Steve Mack and published by Magination Press—explores how grouchy moods impact on oneself and others, and shows simple ways to help.

The Monster at the End of this Book is a Little Golden Book written by Jon Stone and illustrated by Mike Smollin—starring Grover from *Sesame Street*, who throughout the book fears something that he did not need to fear.

The Red Tree by Shaun Tan and published by Hachette Australia—a book about feelings expressed through beautiful artwork, which can be used with older children to explore dark or confusing emotions, depression and hope.

Tough Boris written by Mem Fox, illustrated by Kathryn Brown and published by Penguin Books—explores grief and loss and the reality that everyone feels sad sometimes, through a story about a pirate who loses his pet bird.

Visiting Feelings written by Lauren Rubenstein, illustrated by Shelly Hehenberger and published by Magination Press—encourages children to welcome, notice and explore their emotions, emphasizing that all feelings are okay.

When I'm Feeling…Sad/Angry/Scared/Happy series by Trace Moroney and published by Bonnier Publishing—helpful for psychoeducation about feelings with young children.

Your Fantastic Elastic Brain: Stretch It, Shape It by JoAnn Deak, illustrated by Sarah Ackerley and published by Little Pickle Press—this book teaches children about the brain and, in doing so, explores how important it is to try new things and practice and make mistakes in order to learn new things and improve, including in regard to managing emotions.

Numerous titles by author and illustrator Todd Parr and published by Little, Brown and Company—fun, kind and humorous books about feelings, families, friendships, self-acceptance and more.

Books exploring a variety of different emotions

The Way I Feel by Janan Cain, published by Parenting Press.

My Many Coloured Days by Dr Seuss with paintings by Steve Johnson and Lou Fancher, and published by Random House Children's Publishers.

In My Heart: A Book About Feelings written by Jo Witek, illustrated by Christine Roussey and published by Abrams.

References

Alderson-Day, B. and Fernyhough, C. (2015) 'Inner speech: development, phenomenology, and neurobiology.' *Psychological Bulletin 141*, 5, 931–965.

Attwood, T. (2004) *Exploring Feelings. Cognitive Behavior Therapy to Manage Anxiety.* Texas: Future Horizons.

Attwood, T. and Scarpa, A. (2013) 'Modifications of Cognitive-Behavioral Therapy for Children and Adolescents with High Functioning ASD and Their Common Difficulties.' In A. Scarpa, S. Williams White and T. Attwood (eds) *CBT for Children and Adolescents with High-Functioning Autism Spectrum Disorders.* New York: Guilford Press.

Barrett, P.M. (1999) 'Interventions for child and youth anxiety disorders: involving parents, teachers, and peers.' *Australian Educational and Developmental Psychologist, 16*, 1, 5–24.

Barrett, P., Fisak, B. and Cooper, M. (2015) 'The treatment of anxiety in young children: results of an open trial of the Fun FRIENDS Program.' *Behavior Change 32*, 4, 231–242.

Berk, L. (2013) *Child Development* (9th ed.). Boston: Pearson Education.

Beitchman, J.H., Brownlie, E.B. and Bao, L. (2014) 'Age 31 mental health outcomes of childhood language and speech disorders.' *Journal of the American Academy of Child and Adolescent Psychiatry 53*, 10, 1102–1110.

Bjoroy, A., Madigan, S. and Nylund, D. (2015) 'The Practice of Therapeutic Letter Writing in Narrative Therapy.' In B. Douglas, R. Wolfe, S. Strawbridge, E. Kasket and V. Galbraith (eds) *The Handbook of Counselling Psychology* (4th ed.). London: Sage.

Bostic, J.Q. and King, R.A. (2007) 'Clinical Assessment of Children and Adolescents: Content and Structure.' In A. Martin and F.R. Volkmar (eds) *Lewis's Child and Adolescent Psychiatry: A Comprehensive Textbook* (4th ed.). Philadelphia: Lippincott Williams & Wilkins.

Bratton, S.C. (2015) 'The Empirical Support for Play Therapy: Strengths and Limitations.' In K.J. O'Connor, C.E. Schaefer and L.D. Braverman (eds) *Handbook of Play Therapy.* Hoboken, NJ: John Wiley & Sons.

Bratton, S.C., Ray, D., Rhine, T. and Jones, L. (2005) 'The efficacy of play therapy with children: a meta-analytic review of treatment outcomes.' *Professional Psychology: Research and Practice 36*, 4, 376–390.

Breinholst, S., Esbjorn, B.H., Reinholdt-Dunne, M.L. and Stallard, P. (2012) 'CBT for the treatment of childhood anxiety disorders: a review of why parental involvement has not enhanced outcomes.' *Journal of Anxiety Disorders 26*, 416–424.

Browne, A. (2007) *Silly Billy.* London: Walker Books.

Burns, G.W. (2005) *101 Healing Stories For Kids and Teens: Using Metaphors in Therapy.* Hoboken: John Wiley & Sons.

Burke, C.A. (2010) 'Mindfulness-based approaches with children and adolescents: a preliminary review of current research in an emergent field.' *Journal of Child and Family Studies 19*, 2, 133–144.

Buron, K.D. and Curtis, M. (2013) *The Incredible 5-Point Scale: Assisting Students with Autism Spectrum Disorders in Understanding Social Interactions and Controlling Their Emotional Responses* (2nd ed.). Shawnee Mission: AAPC Pub.

Carr, A. (2012) *Family Therapy: Concepts, Process and Practice* (3rd ed.). Hoboken, NJ: John Wiley & Sons.

Carr, A. (2014a) 'The evidence base for family therapy and systemic interventions for child-focused problems.' *Journal of Family Therapy 36*, 107–157.

Carr, A. (2014b) 'The evidence base for couple therapy, family therapy and systemic interventions for adult-focused problems.' *Journal of Family Therapy 36*, 158–194.

Carr, A. (2016) *The Handbook of Child and Adolescent Clinical Psychology: A Contextual Approach* (3rd rev. ed.). London: Taylor & Francis.

Cassidy, J. and Shaver, P.R. (2016) *Handbook of Attachment: Theory, Research, and Clinical Applications* (3rd ed.). New York: Guilford Press.

Cattanach, A. (2008) *Narrative Approaches to Play with Children.* London: Jessica Kingsley Publishers.

Chen, C., Lawlor, J.P., Duggan, A.K., Hardy, J.B. and Eaton, W.W. (2006) 'Mild cognitive impairment in early life and mental health problems in adulthood.' *American Journal of Public Health 96*, 10, 1772–1778.

Ciarrochi, J., Heaven, P.C.L. and Supavadeeprasit, S. (2008) 'The link between emotion identification skills and socio-emotional functioning in early adolescence: A 1-year longitudinal study.' *Journal of Adolescence 31*, 565–582.

Combrinck-Graham, L. and Fox, G.S. (2007) 'Development of School-Age Children.' In A. Martin and F.R. Volkmar (eds) *Lewis's Child and Adolescent Psychiatry: A Comprehensive Textbook* (4th ed.). Philadelphia: Lippincott Williams & Wilkins.

Cummings, C.M., Caporino, N.E., Settipani, C.A., Read, K.L. *et al.* (2013) 'The therapeutic relationship in cognitive-behavioural therapy and pharmacotherapy for anxious youth.' *Journal of Consulting and Clinical Psychology 81*, 5, 859–864.

David-Ferdon, C. and Kaslow, N.J. (2008) 'Evidence-based psychosocial treatments for child and adolescent depression.' *Journal of Clinical Child and Adolescent Psychology 37*, 1, 62–104.

Dietz, K.R., Lavigne, J.V., Arend, R. and Rosenbaum, D. (1997) 'Relation between intelligence and psychopathology among preschoolers.' *Journal of Clinical Child Psychology 26*, 1, 99–107.

Eisenberg, N., Cumberland, A. and Spinrad, T.L. (1998) 'Parental socialization of emotion.' *Psychological Inquiry 9*, 4, 241–273.

Erikson, E. (2009) *Childhood and Society* (2nd ed.). London: Vintage Publishing. (Original work published 1950.)

Etty-Leal, J. (2010) *Meditation Capsules: A Mindfulness Program for Children.* Melbourne: Meditation Capsules.

Ewing, D.L., Monsen, J.J., Thompson, E.J., Cartwright-Hatton, S. and Field, A. (2015) 'A meta-analysis of transdiagnostic cognitive behavioral therapy in the treatment of child and young person anxiety disorders.' *Behavioral and Cognitive Psychotherapy 43*, 5, 562–577.

Eyberg, S.M., Nelson, M.M. and Boggs, S.R. (2008) 'Evidence-based psychological treatments for children and adolescents with disruptive behavior.' *Journal of Clinical Child and Adolescent Psychology 37*, 1, 215–237.

Faber, A. and Mazlish, E. (2012) *How to Talk So Kids Will Listen and Listen So Kids Will Talk.* New York: Simon and Schuster.

Ford, T., Goodman, R. and Meltzer, H. (2003) 'The British Child and Adolescent Mental Health Survey 1999: the prevalence of DSM-IV Disorders.' *Journal of the American Academy of Child and Adolescent Psychiatry 42*, 1, 1203–1211.

Fox, H. (2003) 'Using therapeutic documents: a review.' *The International Journal of Narrative Therapy and Community Work 4*, 26–36.

Fox, M. and Denton, T. (2005) *Night Noises.* Melbourne: Penguin.

Geldard, K., Geldard, D. and Yin Foo, R. (2013) *Counselling Children: A Practical Introduction* (4th ed.). London: Sage Publications.

Goldenberg, H. and Goldenberg, I. (2013) *Family Therapy: An Overview* (8th ed.) Belmont: BrooksCole Cengage Learning.

Gottman, J.M., Katz, L.F. and Hooven, C. (1997) *Meta-emotion: How Families Communicate Emotionally.* Mahwah: Lawrence Erlbaum Associates.

Grave, J. and Blisset, J. (2004) 'Is cognitive behavior therapy developmentally appropriate for young children: a critical review of the evidence.' *Clinical Psychology Review 24*, 4, 399–420.

Gray, P. (2011) 'The decline of play and the rise of psychopathology in children and adolescents.' *American Journal of Play 3*, 4, 443–463.

Hanh, T.N. (2007) *Planting Seeds: Practicing Mindfulness with Children.* Berkeley: Parallax Press.

Hayes, L., Boyd, C.P. and Sewell, J. (2011) 'Acceptance and commitment therapy for the treatment of adolescent depression: a pilot study in a psychiatric outpatient setting.' *Mindfulness 2*, 2, 86–94.

Hayes, L. and Ciarrochi, J. (2015) *The Thriving Adolescent: Using Acceptance and Commitment Therapy and Positive Psychology to Help Teens Manage Emotions, Achieve Goals, and Build Connection.* Oakland: Context Press.

Havighurst, S.S., Wilson, K.R., Harley, A.E., Kehoe, C., Efron, D. and Prior, M.R. (2013) '"Tuning into Kids": reducing young children's behavior problems using an emotion coaching parenting program.' *Child Psychiatry and Human Development 44*, 2, 247–264.

Havighurst, S.S., Wilson, K.R., Harley, A.E., Prior, M.R. and Kehoe, C. (2010) 'Tuning in to kids: improving emotion socialization practices in parents of preschool children; findings from a community trial.' *Journal of Child Psychology and Psychiatry and Allied Disciplines 51*, 12, 1342–1350.

Hawtin, M. (2013) *Talk Less, Listen More: Solutions for Children's Difficult Behaviors.* Sydney: Ventura Press.

Hearn, J. and Lawrence, M. (1981) 'Family sculpting: 1. Some doubts and some possibilities.' *Journal of Family Therapy 3*, 341–352.

Hearn, J. and Lawrence, M. (1985) 'Family sculpting: 2. Some practical examples.' *Journal of Family Therapy 7*, 113–131.

Henderson, S.W. and Martin, A. (2007) 'Formulation and Integration.' In A. Martin and F.R. Volkmar (eds) *Lewis's Child and Adolescent Psychiatry: A Comprehensive Textbook* (4th ed.). Philadelphia: Lippincott Williams & Wilkins.

Hirshfeld-Becker, D.R., Masek, B., Henin, A., Blakely, L.R. *et al.* (2008) 'Cognitive-behavioral intervention with young anxious children.' *Harvard Review of Psychiatry 16*, 2, 113–125.

Hirshfeld-Becker, D.R., Micco, J.A., Mazursky, H., Bruett, L., and Henin, A. (2011) 'Applying cognitive behavior therapy for anxiety to the younger child.' *Child and Adolescent Clinics of North America 20*, 2, 349–368.

Hobday, A. and Ollier, K. (2005) *Creative Therapy with Children and Adolescents.* Oakland: Impact Publishers.

Howlin, P. and Rutter, M. (1987) 'The Consequences of Language Delay for Other Aspects of Development.' In W. Yule and M. Rutter (eds) *Language Development and Disorders.* London: Mac Keith Press.

Huebner, D. (2005) *What to Do When You Worry Too Much: A Kid's Guide to Overcoming Anxiety.* Washington: Magination Press, APA.

Huebner, D. (2007a) *What to Do When Your Brain Gets Stuck: A Kid's Guide to Overcoming OCD.* Washington: Magination Press, APA.

Huebner, D. (2007b) *What to Do When You Grumble Too Much: A Kid's Guide to Overcoming Negativity.* Washington: Magination Press, APA.

Ironside, V. and Rodgers, F. (2004) *The Huge Bag of Worries.* London: Hachette Children's Group.

Johnson, C.J., Beitchman, J.H. and Brownlie, E.B. (2010) 'Twenty year follow-up of children with and without speech-language impairments: family, educational, occupational and quality of life outcomes.' *American Journal of Speech-Language Pathology 19*, 1, 51–65.

Jongsma Jr., A.E., Peterson, L.M. and McInnis, W.P. (2014) *The Child Psychotherapy Treatment Planner* (5th ed.). New York: Wiley.

Kaiser Greenland, S. (2010) *The Mindful Child.* New York: Atria Paperback.

Karst, P. and Stevenson, G. (2001) *The Invisible String.* Marina Del Rey: DeVorss & Co.

Karver, M.S., Handelsman, J.B., Fields, S. and Bickman, L. (2006) 'Meta-analysis of therapeutic relationship variables in youth and family therapy: the evidence for different relationship variables in the child and adolescent treatment outcome literature.' *Clinical Psychology Review 26*, 1, 50–65.

Kaslow, N.J., Broth, M.R., Smith, C.O. and Collins, M.H. (2012) 'Family-based interventions for child and adolescent disorders.' *Journal of Marital and Family Therapy 38*, 1, 82–100.

Kelsey, S. (2008) 'If I Were a Superhero.' In L. Lowenstein (ed.) *Favorite Therapeutic Activities for Children and Teens: Practitioners Share their Most Effective Interventions.* Toronto: Champion Press.

Kendall, P.C. (ed.) (2006a) *Child and Adolescent Therapy.* New York: The Guilford Press.

Kendall, P.C. (2006b) 'Guiding theory for therapy with children and adolescents.' In P.C. Kendall (ed.) *Child and Adolescent Therapy.* New York: The Guilford Press.

Knell, S.M. (2015) *Cognitive-Behavioral Play Therapy.* Lanham: Rowman & Littlefield Publishers.

Lask, B. (1987) 'Family therapy.' *British Medical Journal 294*, 203–204.

Lawrence, D., Johnson, S., Hafekost, J., Boterhoven De Haan, K., *et al.* (2015) *The Mental Health of Children and Adolescents: Report on the Second Australian Child and Adolescent Survey of Mental Health and Wellbeing.* Canberra: Department of Health.

Livheim, F., Hayes, L., Ghaderi, A., Magnusdottir, T., *et al.* (2015) 'The effectiveness of acceptance and commitment therapy for adolescent mental health: Swedish and Australian pilot outcomes.' *Journal of Child and Family Studies 24*, 4, 1016–1030.

Lowenstein, L. (1999) *Creative Interventions for Troubled Children and Youth.* Toronto: Champion Press.

MacLean, K.L. (2009) *Moody Cow Meditates.* Boston: Wisdom Publications.

Macleod, E., Gross, J. and Hayne, H. (2013) 'The clinical and forensic value of information that children report while drawing.' *Applied Cognitive Psychology 26*, 564–573.

Malchiodi, C.A. (1998) *Understanding Children's Drawings.* New York: The Guilford Press.

Manassis, K., Lee, T.C., Bennett, K., Zhao, X.Y. *et al.* (2014) 'Types of parental involvement in CBT with anxious youth: a preliminary meta-analysis.' *Journal of Consulting and Clinical Psychology 82*, 6, 1163–1172.

March, J. and Benton, C.M. (2006) *Talking Back to OCD: The Program That Helps Kids and Teens say "No Way" and Parents Say "Way to Go."* New York: Guildford Press.

Milner, J. and Bateman, J. (2011) *Working with Children and Teenagers Using Solution Focused Approaches.* London: Jessica Kingsley Publishers.

Nichols, M.P. (2011) *The Essentials of Family Therapy.* Boston, MA: Pearson.

Pahl, K.M. and Barrett, P.M. (2010) 'Preventing anxiety and promoting social and emotional strength in preschool children: a universal evaluation of the Fun FRIENDS program.' *Advances in School Mental Health Promotion 3*, 3, 14–25.

Perry, B., Hogan, L. and Marlin, S. (2000) 'Curiosity, pleasure and play: a neurodevelopmental perspective.' *HAAEYC Advocate*, August, 9–12.

Peterson, L. and Adderley, A. (2002) *Stop Think Do: Social Skills Training—Early Years of Schooling Ages 4–8.* Melbourne: ACER.

Piaget, J. (1962a) 'The stages of the intellectual development of the child.' *Bulletin of the Menninger Clinic 26*, 120–128.

Piaget, J. (1962b) 'The relation of affectivity to intelligence in the mental development of the child.' *Bulletin of the Menninger Clinic 26*, 129–137.

Pincus. D.B. (2011) *I Can Relax! A Relaxation CD for Children.* A product of the Child Anxiety Network. Released 18 January. Psychzone Inc.

Rapee, R., Lyneham, H., Schniering, C., Wuthrich, V. *et al.* (2006) *Cool Kids Anxiety Program.* Sydney: Centre for Emotional Health.

Retzlaff, R., von Sydow, K., Beher, S., Haun, M.W. and Schweitzer, J. (2013) 'The efficacy of systemic therapy for internalizing and other disorders of childhood and adolescence: a systematic review of 38 randomized trials.' *Family Process 52*, 4, 619–652.

Reynolds, S., Wilson, C., Austin, J. and Hooper, L. (2012) 'Effects of psychotherapy for children and adolescents: a meta-analytic review.' *Clinical Psychology Review 32*, 4, 251–262.

Rieffe, C. and Rooij. M. (2012) 'The longitudinal relationship between emotion awareness and internalizing symptoms during late childhood.' *European Child and Adolescent Psychiatry 21*, 6, 349–356.

Romain, T. and Verdick, E. (2000) *Stress Can Really Get On Your Nerves.* Minneapolis: Free Spirit Publishing.

Ronen, T. (1997) *Cognitive Developmental Therapy with Children.* Chichester: Wiley.

Scarpa, A., Williams White, S. and Attwood, T. (eds) (2013) *CBT for Children and Adolescents with High Functioning Autism Spectrum Disorders.* New York: The Guilford Press.

Schaffer, H.R. (2004) *Introducing Child Psychology.* Oxford: Blackwell Publishing.

Shirk, R.S. and Karver, M. (2003) 'Prediction of treatment outcome from relationship variables in child and adolescent therapy: a meta-analytic review.' *Journal of Consulting and Clinical Psychology 71*, 3, 452–464.

Siegel, D. and Bryson, T.P. (2012) *The Whole-Brain Child: 12 Revolutionary Strategies to Nurture Your Child's Development, Survive Everyday Parenting Struggles, and Help Your Family Thrive.* New York: Delacorte Press.

Siegel, D.J. and Hartzell, M. (2014) *Parenting from the Inside Out: How a Deeper Self-understanding Can Help You Raise Children Who Thrive.* London: Scribe Publications.

Silverman, W.K., Pina, A.A. and Viswesvaran, C. (2008) 'Evidence-based psychosocial treatments for phobic and anxiety disorders in children and adolescents.' *Journal of Clinical Child and Adolescent Psychology 37*, 1, 105–130.

Snel, E. (2013) *Sitting Still Like a Frog: Mindfulness Exercises for Kids (and Their Parents).* Boulder, CO: Shambhala Publications.

Sofronoff, K., Attwood, T. and Hinton, S. (2005) 'A randomized controlled trial of a CBT intervention for anxiety in children with Asperger syndrome.' *Journal of Child Psychology and Psychiatry 46*, 11, 1152–1160.

Sosinsky, L.S., Gilliam, W.S. and Mayes, L.C. (2007) 'The Preschool Child.' In A. Martin and F.R. Volkmar (eds) *Lewis's Child and Adolescent Psychiatry: A Comprehensive Textbook* (4th ed.). Philadelphia: Lippincott Williams & Wilkins.

Špinka, M., Newberry, R.C. and Bekoff, M. (2001) 'Mammalian play: training for the unexpected.' *The Quarterly Review of Biology 76*, 2, 141–168.

Stallard, P. (2002) *Think Good—Feel Good: A Cognitive-Behavioral Therapy Workbook for Children and Young People.* Chichester: Wiley.

Stallard, P. (2013) 'Adapting cognitive behaviour therapy for children and adolescents.' In P. Graham and S. Reynolds (eds) *Cognitive Behavior Therapy for Children and Families* (3rd ed.). Cambridge: Cambridge University Press.

Stern, M.B. (2008) *Child-Friendly Therapy: Biopsychosocial Innovations for Children and Families*. New York: Norton.

Swain, J., Hancock, K., Dixon, A. and Bowman, J. (2015) 'Acceptance and commitment therapy for children: a systematic review of intervention studies.' *Journal of Contextual Behavioral Science 4*, 73–85.

Thomas, B. (2009) *Creative Coping Skills for Children. Emotional Support through Arts and Crafts Activities*. London: Jessica Kingsley Publishers.

Ung, D., Selles, R., Small, B.J. and Storch, E.A. (2015) 'A systematic review and meta-analysis of cognitive-behavioral therapy for anxiety in youth with high-functioning autism spectrum disorders.' *Child Psychiatry and Human Development 46*, 4, 533–547.

von Sydow, K., Retzlaff, R., Beher, S., Haun, M.W. and Schweitzer, J. (2013) 'The efficacy of systemic therapy for childhood and adolescent externalizing disorders: a systematic review of 47 RCT.' *Family Process 52*, 4, 576–618.

Wellman, H.M., Hollander, M. and Schult, C.A. (1996) 'Young children's understanding of thought bubbles and of thoughts.' *Child Development 67*, 3, 768–788.

Wever, C. and Phillips, N. (1996) *The School Wobblies*. Sydney: Shrink-Rap Press.

White, M. and Epston, D. (1990) *Narrative Means to Therapeutic Ends*. New York: Norton.

White, M. and Morgan, A. (2006) *Narrative Therapy with Children and Their Families*. Adelaide: Dulwich Centre Publications.

Whitehouse, E. and Pudney, W. (1998) *A Volcano in My Tummy: Helping Children to Handle Anger*. Gabriola Island: New Society Publishers.

Willard, C. (2010) *Child's Mind: Mindfulness Practices to Help Our Children Be More Focused, Calm, and Relaxed*. Berkeley: Parallax Press.

Woolford, J., Patterson, T., Macleod, E., Hobbs, L. and Hayne, H. (2015) 'Drawing helps children to talk about their presenting problems during a mental health assessment.' *Clinical Child Psychology and Psychiatry 20*, 1, 68–83.

Vygotsky, L. (1966) 'Play and its role in the mental development of the child.' *Soviet Psychology 5*, 3, 6–18.

Yew, S.G. and O'Kearny, R. (2013) 'Emotional and behavioral outcomes later in childhood and adolescence for children with specific language impairments: meta-analyses of controlled prospective studies.' *Journal of Child Psychology and Psychiatry 54*, 5, 516–524.

Zelazo, P.D. and Lyons, K.E. (2011) 'Mindfulness training in childhood.' *Human Development 54*, 2, 61–65.

Dr Fiona Zandt works in private practice and as a Senior Clinical Psychologist with the Specialist Autism Team at the Royal Children's Hospital, Melbourne. She is a guest lecturer at a number of universities.

Dr Suzanne Barrett works in private practice providing clinical psychology services to children, adolescents and families, as well as supervision to psychologists and clinical psychology registrars.

Together, Fiona and Suzanne facilitate practical training workshops for therapists working with children. For more information, visit www.childpsychologyworkshops.com.au